D0866627

JOAN CHITTISTER

Joan Chittister

In My Own Words

Compiled and Edited
by Mary Lou Kownacki

Liguori
LIGUORI, MISSOURI

Imprimi Potest:
Thomas D. Picton, C.Ss.R.
Provincial, Denver Province
The Redemptorists

Published by Liguori Publications
Liguori, Missouri
To order, call 800-325-9521
www.liguori.org

Introduction and compilation © 2008 by Mary Lou Kownacki

All rights reserved. No part of this publication may be reproduced, stored in a retrieval system, or transmitted in any form or by any means—electronic, mechanical, photocopy, recording, or any other—except for brief quotations in printed reviews, without the prior written permission of the publisher.

Library of Congress Cataloging-in-Publication Data

Chittister, Joan.
    In my own words / Joan Chittister ; compiled and edited by Mary Lou Kownacki.
      p. cm.
    ISBN 978-0-7648-1753-3
    1. Chittister, Joan. 2. Christian life—Catholic authors. 3. Catholic Church—Doctrines. I. Kownacki, Mary Lou. II. Title.
BX4705.C476A25 2008
271'.97—dc22

                    2008025251

Scripture citations are taken from the New Revised Standard Version of the Bible, copyright 1989 by the Division of Christian Education of the National Council of the Churches of Christ in the USA. All rights reserved. Used with permission.

Excerpts from *Heart of Flesh* (1998), *Scarred by Struggle, Transformed by Hope* (2003), *The Story of Ruth* (2000), and *Welcome to the Wisdom of the World* (2007), all authored by Joan Chittister, reprinted by permission of the publisher, Wm. B. Eerdmans Publishing Company, Grand Rapids, MI, copyright © in years indicated; all rights reserved.

Excerpts from *Praying with the Benedictines: A Window on the Cloister*, by Guerric DeBona. Copyright © 2007 by Paulist Press. Paulist Press Inc., New York/Mahwah, NJ. Reprinted by permission of Paulist Press, Inc. www.paulistpress.com.

Liguori Publications, a nonprofit corporation, is an apostolate of the Redemptorists. To learn more about the Redemptorists, visit Redemptorists.com.

Printed in the United States of America
12 11 10 09 08   5 4 3 2 1
First edition

CONTENTS

$\mathcal{A}$CKNOWLEDGMENTS

"No duty," Saint Ambrose wrote, "is more urgent than that of returning thanks."

I write these simple thank you notes with a sense of urgency.

Abundant thanks to Carolyn Gorny-Kopkowski, Rosanne Lindal-Hynes, and Mary Miller, my friends and Benedictine sisters—the Golden Girls as we call ourselves—for spending many hours cutting and pasting hundreds of excerpts from hundreds of sources that I had photocopied, and for meticulously labeling them with dates, titles, and page numbers.

I relied heavily, as I always do, on Anne McCarthy, OSB and Mary Miller, OSB for a first reading of all collected materials. They made astute, though difficult, choices but assured me that I have enough material left for second book. I would like to thank them for their time, the close reading, and sound advice.

Next I would like to thank Alicia von Stamwitz, my editor from Liguori, who contacted me about the project, encouraged me, extended my deadlines, and then did a second reading. Again, some hard decisions were needed, and she tells me that I have enough material left for a third book. Alicia is an excellent editor, and this was an enriching and enjoyable experience for me.

I am also grateful to Annmarie Sanders, IHM, communications director for the Leadership Conference of Women Religious, who did an outstanding job of capturing Joan in a power-point presentation when Joan received the 2007 Outstanding Leadership Award from the LCWR. I used a couple of quotes from that presentation in the introduction. And a final thanks to the student who came to Mount Saint Benedict Monastery in Erie, PA from Ohio Wesleyan College as part of a group live-in experience and spent the day helping in our inner-city ministries. She ended up with me. Thanks for all the copying.

Most of all I would like to thank my friend and co-worker, Susan Doubet, OSB, who is one of Joan Chittister's assistants. It is impossible for me to imagine doing this project without Susan. First, she has indexed and organized all of Joan Chittister's writings so locating them was effortless. Then she supplied me with an outline and neatly filed copies of magazine articles, interviews, book chapters, as well as the books themselves. After I read through the materials, and my friends and I cut and pasted my selections, she performed the Herculean task of finding my choices on hard drive and transmitting them to manuscript form. I owe her big time, and I'm sure she won't let me forget it.

$\mathcal{I}$NTRODUCTION

I know Joan Chittister as prioress, sister, mentor, and friend of 40 years.

We taught high school together, ventured into the dangerous countryside of Haiti to document human rights abuses, swam with stingrays in the Caribbean, and continue to trigger each others' imaginations for book ideas and new projects. We worked together on publications for 25 years; I have read the drafts of all her books and edited numerous publications by her. I consider these years a privilege, gift, and responsibility.

The point is I thought I knew Joan quite well. If asked to give a word description of her, I would have offered one of following: passion, energy, compassion, leader, visionary, prophet. But after putting this book together—reading over 30 published books, hundreds of articles, dozens of chapters in other books, countless interviews, and her monthly newsletter of 17 years—the only authentic word to describe Joan is "Seeker." She is a woman in quest. She probes the hard questions, forges new answers, and exposes the reasons behind the reasons people give for doing things that no longer work.

Maybe I shouldn't have been surprised. After all, she titled the Festschrift published by Orbis on her 65th birthday, *Spiritual Questions for the 21st Century.* And her spiritual memoir published by Sheed & Ward is titled *Called to Question.* Still, I was unprepared for the propelling impact of her questions in everything I read.

There was no choice, then, but to compile this book into the questions that steered Joan's life and the themes emerging from that quest.

That said, it would be a mistake to picture Joan as someone who sits at a computer and postures questions as a philosophical or theological exercise. All her questions erupt out of lived experience. She explained, "I simply say out loud the questions that are bothering people everywhere, eating out their hearts and eroding their commitment to both Church and state." To say the unspoken question aloud is a rare gift. And a dangerous one. Questions threaten those in power.

Why did she start to question if a Christian could support war? Joan reports that it was when her young cousin died in Vietnam, and at the same time, some of her Benedictine friends were going to jail to protest war. Chittister became a public spokesperson for the Catholic peace moment, a move that she termed personally "cataclysmic" because it thrust her out of "good sister" circles and edged her to the margins.

"What is the purpose of religious life?" she wondered, as babies were napalmed on TV, snarling dogs attacked blacks in the streets of Selma, and choral prayer droned on in chapel. After intense personal struggle, she concluded: "The world needs contemplative women who see the world as God sees the world and so critique any system, either Church or state, that denies any people the fullness of creation." She then worked tirelessly to redefine and renew contemporary religious life as a transforming agent that confronted both castle and cathedral with the "foolish standards of the gospel."

The seeds of the women's question were planted in childhood when Joan's recently widowed young mother entered a second marriage that was often volatile and precarious. When Joan begged her mother to leave her stepfather, her mother answered, "There is nothing else a woman can do, Joan." Though undereducated and economically dependent, Joan's mother had a brilliant mind and trained her only child fiercely for independence. What she could not have, she wanted for her daughter. Joan states, "I grew up with this question in the center of my soul: "Why all this diminishment of women?" She carried that question anywhere women were invisible or diminished—into corporate boardrooms, chanceries, government halls, and the Vatican.

"What is sin?" she asked. And in the midst of the Church's call for a "fundamental option for the poor," she answered: "The sin to be repented, amended, eradicated was the great systemic sin against God's little ones. For that kind of sin, in my silence, I had become deeply guilty." The question of institutional sin plunged her into the depths of human deprivation, poverty, hunger, war, and trafficking of women. Forging friendships with God's poor and taking personal responsibility to plead their cases, she traveled into the slums and war zones of South Africa, Palestine, Israel, Haiti, India, China, the Philippines, Mexico, and the Soviet Union.

To give import to questions like these demands a public platform. Blessed with a sharp and analytical mind, an educational background in leadership theory, a passionate and powerful voice, and a magnetic charisma that attracts trust and confidence, Joan found herself thrust at an early age into leadership positions that enabled her to press these questions on podiums and in print.

As president of her Benedictine federation, president of the Leadership Conference of Women Religious, and prioress of the Benedictine Sisters of Erie, she seized the public forum to unify and empower groups to be more than they ever thought possible. She soon found herself in an international spotlight—entering debates on national television, giving interviews to major publications, and responding to hundreds of speaking requests.

An electrifying preacher, Joan brought packed audiences around the world to their feet, igniting them with new hope and vision. One interviewer wrote, "The sheer authority of her voice and the force of her indictment made me feel as if I were being pressed back against my plush, red-cushioned seat, as when a plane takes off."

Her writings equaled the impact of her preaching. She became a prolific, award-winning author whose books on monastic, feminist and contemporary spirituality are already listed as "classics." All of these works cemented what one reviewer called "a wisdom that comes only from a life well-lived and a carefully cultivated spirituality."

Although I believe the scope and breadth of her work will place her in history with great Benedictine luminaries like Hildegard of Bingen, my favorite part of this book was editing the chapters that dealt with Joan as human being. I wanted readers to know that Joan is known as much for her extravagant heart, outrageous humor, and largess of spirit as for her abundant works. A gifted listener and compassionate presence, she has the rare ability to make each individual feel accepted, understood, and valued.

Dena Merriam, convener of the Global Peace Initiative for Women that Joan co-chairs, writes: "I have sat by her side as she mediated the emotional tirades of Israeli and Palestinian women. I have looked to her to calm the turmoil as Iraqi Shia and Sunni came together for dialogue—and her presence was able to cut through the storm of anger that had taken hold of the group. I have seen her compassion and tears as she held Iraqi refuges in Syria. Her heart has taken them all in. They won't forget her and she won't forget them."

"Being taken into Joan's heart" is an experience shared by countless persons undergoing spiritual struggles, sickness, abandonment, rejection, and loss. And much of her great heart comes through in her writings.

But great blessings bring great burdens and Chittister is no exception. The power of her personality and relentless questioning make her a lightning rod in Church and in community, wherever two or three gather. As much as she is admired, applauded and honored, she is also criticized, vilified, and rejected. I have seen her at the heights of ovations and accolades. I have witnessed her pained, angry, bitter and depressed over church, world, and community affairs. And I have seen her put ideas on ice by lashing out with a few frozen words when the darkness of that space overcomes. That she is as flawed as any human being goes without saying.

But here's the crux: She endures. Tirelessly she trumpets a testimony of hope against the vise of death. And women, the poor, seekers, and the disenfranchised everywhere are richer for it. Joan has written, "The commitment to question every aspect of the human journey is the only form of fidelity worth the price of admission to this sojourn called life."

Joan continues to pursue her questions like a mole in winter ground tunneling toward dawn. We can do no less. Let us join Joan in prayer for the grace to pursue our own questions and the courage to face the consequences.

May your journey
through these questions
bring you to a new moment
of awareness.

May it be an enlightening one.

May you find,
like all the students of life before you,
the answers you yourself are seeking now.

May they awaken in you
that which is deeper than fact,
truer than fiction,
full of faith.

May you come to know
that in every human event
is a particle of the Divine
to which we turn
for meaning here,
to which we tend
for fullness of life hereafter.

WELCOME TO THE
WISDOM OF THE WORLD

Opposite: Joan Chittister, 2005.
Photograph by Ed Bernik.
Courtesy Benetvision.

CHAPTER I

WHAT DO I BELIEVE?

My family was a fishing family.

I grew up with it: sitting on the public dock all day Saturday, camped out on the grassy lowlands of the old Soldiers and Sailors home after school at night, one hand on a book, the other on my line.

Even after I went to the monastery, I fished. "Do you ever catch anything?" people said with amazement, a touch of the incredulous, a hint of the patronizing in their tone of voice. "I've never missed a sunset yet," I said.

It took years before even I knew what I was saying. The truth is that I didn't really fish at all. None of us did: Dad sat and watched the waves; Mom sat and thought. I sat and wrote poetry in my head. We all just went and sat near the water where it was legitimate to be silent, or floated down a lagoon where it was impossible to go anywhere, or drifted around over an old wreck about 100 yards off shore that sank into the swell of the water, the massive power of being helpless and secure at the same time.

It took years before I realized that this point was the actual endpoint of all the years of prayer, all the days of scripture study, all the devotions and exercises and Mass attendance and holy days I'd spent "searching for God." This was really what they had all been about: They weren't about loading a stringer with perch. They were about sinking into the arms of God and realizing finally that that was enough.

THE MONASTIC WAY

One day, in second grade, I'm told that Protestants don't go to Heaven. Well, I was stunned. I was the only child in that class who didn't have a Catholic mother and Catholic father. Mixed marriages, that euphemism for crossing boundaries, just didn't exist and the local parish priest railed against them.

Well, I raced out of school that night. I did not stay to clean the board. I didn't carry out the waste paper basket. I didn't do papers for Sister. I just shot out of there. My mother was in the kitchen doing dishes and I just raced into the kitchen. I had to talk to my mother alone, and I wanted that question out of the way. My mother looked at me, "What happened to you? You're certainly excited. What's going on? Did something new happen in school today? What did you learn in school today that's got you so excited?" I looked at her, and I said to her right up, "Today I learned that Protestants don't go to Heaven." And my mother didn't move. She didn't say anything. She just went on at the sink and then she said very quietly, "And what do you think about that, Joan?" And I said, "I think it's wrong. I think Sister is wrong." My mother turned around from the sink, and I could see her body, but I didn't know what was going to happen. She turned around and said, "Why do you think Sister is wrong?" I thought for a minute and I said, "Sister doesn't know Daddy." She didn't have all the information, you see. Sister would never be wrong if somebody had told her all the information. So it was clear that she had never seen anything like this. So my mother, I can still see her, she's wiping her hands on her apron and puts her arms around me and pulls me over and she says, "What did you say to Sister, Joan?" And I remember, even telling this story now, I remember the shame. And I said, "I didn't say anything." And my mother hugged me against her stomach, her hard little stomach, and she said, "You're a very bright little girl, and I'm proud of you, Joan. You don't have to say anything now. You can tell Sister later." Honest to God, I think I've spent my whole life waiting to tell people how wrong this was.

I was affected by it negatively as a child and yet out of that negative experience and pressure, came a positive drive to kind of eliminate it from my own life—not to be part of any religion that somehow or other was the oppressor of others, of another religion. And I suppose it's because I certainly made a judgment that my stepfather's family was good and so who was I as a Catholic or anything else to judge them negatively? I simply decided I was not going to be part of that. I simply withdrew from that as a seven or eight-year-old child. I had no power in the system; I had no voice in the system. I had nothing, but down deep in me, I knew.

And it's shaped my life. I spent my whole life with a foot on each side of the fence, and I absolutely refused to move either foot.

BEING CATHOLIC NOW

I grew up among competent women—my mother, the sisters at school. I saw them as splendid role models. Then I began to discover that competence is not enough.

I tell a story about wanting to be an altar girl when I was in grade school. First, I memorized all the prayers in Latin. Then I answered the next appeal for altar boys.

When I stayed after school on the appointed afternoon, Sister said to me, "Joan, did you want something?" "Sister," I said, "I'd like to be an altar boy." "Joan, you can't be an altar boy." "Yes, I can," I told her, "I know all the prayers." I began to recite them to prove it. Nobody wanted to know. I could hear the boys snicker and I knew not one of them knew the prayers the way I did.

I remember wanting to give my whole life to the Church, to the people of God. Not necessarily as a priest—I don't think I have a call to priesthood. But I believe some women do, however, and I think I can speak for them with a special kind of authenticity, because I'm not speaking for myself. When I found that a complete commitment to the Church was denied to women because they are women, I carried that hurt inside me for a long time.

TODAY'S PARISH MAGAZINE
OCTOBER 1984
INTERVIEW WITH CAROL CLARKE

As a young teenager, kneeling in a dark cathedral one night, with no illumination in the church but the sanctuary lamp, I had an experience of intense light. I was thirteen years old and totally convinced that, whatever it was and wherever it came from, the light was God. Perhaps it was a good janitor working late, or a bad switch that did not work at all, or a startling insight given to a young woman, given gratuitously. I did not know then and I do not know now. But I did know that the light was God and that God was light.

GOD AT 2000

My months in a polio hospital were some of the most devastating, most meaningful of my life. I was only sixteen when the disease struck and a life of unremitting disability seemed, on hard days, to be more than I could bear. No one knew if I would ever walk again. No one knew what, if anything, I would be able to do to make a living. No one could guarantee that I would get better. Nor did anyone try. And worse, whatever the sense of isolation, I was not alone in the dread and agony of polio's unknowables. Some people there, I realized—quarantined, bored by the interminable waiting for therapies and cures and help that never came—were more crippled by depression than by paralysis. Others railed daily at the thought of being restrained in any way. A few worked day and night to no avail against the ravages of the disease and got quieter and quieter as the months went by.

But there were two fellows in the ward at the end of the hall who made all the difference: Every day at ten o'clock, just as the staff began to meet for consultations, they rolled from room to room in their wheelchairs organizing the daily wheelchair race in the hall. They gave points and prizes and long applause to the winners. It was weeks before I got up the energy to join them but when I look back now, I realize that the day I did was the day I began to get well.

SCARRED BY STRUGGLE,
TRANSFORMED BY HOPE

I had wanted to be a sister for as long as I could remember. Long before I started school I knew where life would eventually lead. By the time I was in high school, I had begun the long and arduous process of community hunting.

Then, one night, just as I was leaving the Academy grounds, I became conscious of the sound of the chant coming out of the second-floor chapel windows as I never had heard it before. It was pure as spun steel, high and rhythmic and unending. It swirled through the yard and caught me up in itself and put me down on the other side of my decision. It was obvious; the music was the answer. Somewhere deep inside me I knew what I had known all the time: In the end, I would follow the music.

I'd been playing the piano for ten years. When nothing else calmed me or stirred my soul, music did.

To this day, I am fond of telling people who ask me what my day is like that I live life between two keyboards. The one, my computer, sits at the end of my desk and empties my soul. The other, my keyboard, sits at the end of the desk, and when the day is too long or the empty page too daunting, fills it up again. No doubt about it: Music brought me to the monastery as surely as any description of the community's ministries did.

LISTEN WITH THE HEART

It has not always been easy—I went through a terrible period as a young sister—to the point that I thought I would have to leave religious life because I doubted the divinity of Jesus. Only when I realized that I did believe deeply and profoundly in God could I come to peace with the fact that faith in God would have to be enough. It was a dark, empty time. It threw me back on the barest of beliefs but the deepest of beliefs. I hung on in hope like a spider on a thread. But the thread was enough for me. As a result, my faith actually deepened over the years. The humanity of Jesus gave promise to my own. Jesus ceased to be distant and ethereal and "perfect." Jesus let no system, no matter how revered, keep him from a relationship with God. And that union with God, I came to understand, was divine. Then I also understood that questions are of the essence in a mature faith.

I don't fear my questions any more. I know that they are all part of the process of coming to union with God and refusing to make an idol of anything less. The point is that during that difficult time I didn't try to force anything. I simply lived in the desert believing that whatever life I found there was life enough for me. I believed that God was in the darkness. It is all part of the purification process and should be revered. It takes away from us our paltry little definitions of God and brings us face-to-face with the Transcendent. It is not to be feared. It is simply to be experienced. Then, God begins to live in us without benefit of recipes and rituals, laws and "answer"—of which there are, in the final analysis, none at all.

IN A DARK WOOD

I myself had entered a monastery intent on finding what, I learned later, earlier seekers had called "spiritual consolations." I wanted to "find God." I wanted to be "holy." I wanted to "get to heaven." Most of all, I wanted to feel good about the state of my soul. I wanted a life that was separate from the world, apart from the fray, above the grimy reality of the begging lepers and threatening strangers and bold women and grubby outcasts who populated the Gospels. Surely a monastic life was the way to do that quickly.

But it didn't work.

I began to discover that monastic life itself was basically a routine of good practices designed to open us to the possibility of finding God. But it did not guarantee it. It was all about possibility, not promise. It was not a sure trick or a quick fix. It was, at best, only the means, not the end.

So, as the years went by, I found myself in the kind of confusion which, I came later to understand, makes the spiritual real. The temple preached a message I did not yet see—even in the temple itself: in a country full of temples the hungry among us were still starving. Too many children were sick and uneducated. The poor were dying without care.

Even the temples themselves had no room for half of creation. Women were never accepted as full members, were always invisible, were forever dismissed—as useless but useful, a kind of heavenly mistake, functional, of course, but not fully human. In many temples, blacks were segregated and homosexuals were chastised, and those the temples called "sinful" were shunned.

Obedience had become the central virtue; law was whatever the system defined. And all the while holy disobedience was what was really needed.

In a country we called "Christian," the Jesus story had become more fancy than fact.

Then, in the 1960s, the Second Vatican Council and its aftermath called the church, the whole people of God, even the keepers of the temple, to a cataclysmic examination of conscience. From inside the temple, and because of the temple, my whole life was put in question.

Suddenly, the new institutional examination of conscience made sense. All of life had erupted in one great burst of understanding that no amount of regularity and order could possibly bring. There was a world out there that was itself "the heart of the temple." It was now a matter of bringing the temple to the world and the world to the heart of it.

IN THE HEART OF THE TEMPLE

Thomas Merton changed my attitude toward monasticism. I began to realize that the role of the monastic was to confront the world with the questions of the world, not with the questions of some esoteric monastery chapter meeting, let alone the seminary theology tests.

VISION MAGAZINE
OCTOBER 1996
INTERVIEW WITH
REV. JOSEPH J. DRISCOLL

Exhausted by the spiritual wrenching that came with having lived through a "good war" and now watching as we ourselves conducted an evil one, I became part of a Christian peace movement that challenged the continuing viability of any theory of a just war in a world where disproportionality was now official government policy and discrimination in targeting a theological joke. The questions simply would not, could not, quit in me. The personal effects of the spiritual scuffle were cataclysmic for me.

Once a very standard-brand U.S. Roman Catholic, I now found myself inside some new circles and outside some old ones. I was suddenly considered "radical" to most, "communist" to some, at best "misguided" to many, including priests who previously had called me "a good sister." But there was no turning back. The gentle Jesus of my daily prayer was far too clear to be ignored at a time of social convenience. I found myself certain that though conflict resolution might not be able to guarantee peace, violence certainly could not. Violence launched for the sake of political ends was a sin. It lurked under false pretenses of honor and righteousness but it was evil. And the seed of it lived in my own soul or no government would ever be able to tap it there so easily for the sake of its crusades and inquisitions and carpet bombings and ethnic cleansings and genocides.

Systemic violence was not holy, and I could not support any country that was doing it, not even my own; and further, Scripture showed me quite clearly, never, ever, could I give such support in the name of Jesus.

SPIRITUAL QUESTIONS
FOR THE 21ST CENTURY

It happened only once but it affected me for the rest of my life. In 1976, the Vatican issued its first explanation for the non-ordination of women. Why, women asked, could good, committed, spiritual, baptized women not also be priests? Because, Rome said, women didn't look like men. End of discussion. End of theological development. End of consistency of the faith. But it was also the beginning of an entirely new flood of questions. As in, Is the Eucharist an event of the Christian community or simply a drama we are replaying? Do we celebrate Eucharist "in remembrance of Him" or in imitation of Him? Did Jesus "become flesh" as in fully human, or did Jesus simply become male, as in a particular gender and for the sake of that gender?

It isn't that I hadn't struggled with those questions for years. In fact, I burned inside at the high-handedness of such a non-response to such serious theological concerns. Most of all, as then president of the largest group of women religious in the world, I was empowered—expected, in fact—to speak on their behalf for the concerns of women everywhere. But I didn't. Not really. I spoke, of course. But in a way that completely ignored the inconsistency of the answer. Instead, my official response was short and bland; oh, very true, yes, but very, very political. The statement I put out said, "Now that we understand what the issue is we can study it." It was the perfect answer of the perfect victim in the face of perfect power. It was "nice." It wasn't "aggressive." It did everything but whimper. And it did nothing at all to advance the question of the role of women in the Church or to invite dialogue.

The consternation on the faces of the women who came to talk to me about the public statement said it all. For political reasons, I explained—in the hope of being able to pursue the question and at the same time not to split the conference over an issue that was not only not yet vital to every member but even confusing to many—I had said nothing. I had opted to save the organization rather than to "speak truth to power." And in that act, truth as I knew it in the depths of me wasted away.

I knew then and there that I would never do that again. I would never again squander the tiny space a woman has to say anything of value. I had played at mock peacemaking where there was no peace. I had failed to claim my own power and in that failure failed to empower others, as well.

CALLED TO QUESTION

Benedictines read the Scriptures every day and reflect on how to relate them to the modern world. That has been a very, very important part of learning to see through Christ's eyes for me. I read the Gospels and notice how Christ treats the outcasts and listen to how he responds to the social questions of his day.

Some of the questions are variations of those we humans face today. Is AIDS a curse from God? Well, a man asked Jesus about a blind man, "Rabbi, who sinned? The man or his parents?" And Jesus said, "Neither. This man was born blind so that God's glory could shine forth in healing him." Those words tell me that Christ looks at sickness as something to heal, not to use against a person. Then I ask myself, "Well, who are the outcasts of my day and what is my attitude toward them? What are the major social concerns of my world, and how might Jesus respond to them?"

I have this little private theory that may work only for myself, but I like to use it. I imagine I won't die until I've had an opportunity to live all of the dimensions of the human condition as presented by Scripture. And, for instance, when I feel a terrible anger about something, I'll say to myself, "Well, which Scripture am I living now?" And sometimes I find I'm living out the story of Samson. Then I have a choice to make just as he did. Am I going to pull the ceiling down on myself as well as on all these other people, as Samson did? If so, what have I proven, what have I accomplished?

U.S. CATHOLIC
SEPTEMBER 1988
INTERVIEW WITH EDITORS

"Why does a woman like you stay in the Church?" a woman asked me from the depths of a dark audience years ago. "Because," I answered, "every time I thought about leaving, I found myself thinking of oysters." "Oysters?" she said. "What do oysters have to do with it?" "Well," I answered her in the darkness of the huge auditorium, "I realized that an oyster is an organism that defends itself by excreting a substance to protect itself against the sand of its spawning bed. The more sand in

the oyster, the more chemical the oyster produces until finally, after layer upon layer of gel, the sand turns into a pearl. And the oyster itself becomes more valuable in the process. At that moment," I said, "I discovered the ministry of irritation."

LUTHERAN WOMAN TODAY
OCTOBER 1996

I know the transition from certainty to faith, from faithful answers to faithful questions. I have gone through it myself. So when I pray, I still say "I believe," but the truth is that I now believe both a great deal less and a great deal more than I did years ago. I believe a great deal less about the historical or scientific dimensions of the faith and a great deal more about the mystery of creation, the ongoing struggle of redemption and the commonplace of sanctity. And furthermore, I believe that just about everybody else does, too.

IN SEARCH OF BELIEF

Opposite: Joan Chittister and Iraqi woman refugee in Syria, 2006. Photograph by Janelle Surpris. Courtesy Benetvision.

CHAPTER 2

WHAT DOES IT MEAN TO BE HUMAN?

The human being is a creature-in-search whose eternal compass is set to the interminable question "For what?" For what are we really searching in life? Where should we go to seek it? How will we know when we have found it?

The questions ring across time, through great literature, in popular music, behind every major work of art. Every culture, every spirituality, every wisdom figure in every arena of life concentrates on finding the answer to the secret of living, the endpoint of life. Whatever the magnet that draws them on, whatever the tradition that guides them, these seekers walk the same way, they beat a single path, and eventually they come to the same conclusion.

"The meaning of life is to see," as a Chinese proverb teaches.

"Listen," the ancient Rule of Benedict instructs.

"The real voyage of discovery consists not in seeking new landscapes," the philosopher Marcel Proust writes, "but in having new eyes."

It is not, in other words, so much where we go in life that matters, it is the way in which we immerse ourselves in it, open ourselves to it, see beyond its trappings wherever we are that measures the quality of the journey.

GRACE IS EVERYWHERE
AFTERWORD

What do I define as human? I believe in the pursuit of the spiritual, presence to pain, and the sacredness of life. Without these, life is useless and humanity a farce.

WHAT DOES IT MEAN TO BE HUMAN?

We are put here to love, not for the sake of the other alone, but for our own sakes as well. To dare to love another as a person, rather than as an idea, is to turn ourselves over to be shaped and reshaped in life. The people who love us do for us what we cannot do for ourselves. They release the best in us; they shoulder us through the rough times in life; they stretch us beyond the confines of our own experiences to wider visions, to truer vistas. They show us the face of our creating, caring God on earth.

Perhaps the deepest spiritual understanding we can muster here is that human love is the only proof we have of the love of God. It is also the only arms God has with which to love us here and now, clearly and warmly, joyfully and achingly.

CALLED TO QUESTION

To be human it is necessary to think again about what matters in life. We must ask always why what is, is. To be human is to listen to the rest of the world with a tender heart, and learn to live life with our arms open and our souls seared with a sense of responsibility for everything that is.

Without a doubt, given that criteria, we may indeed not live the "better life," but we may, at the end, at least have lived a fully human one.

WHAT DOES IT MEAN TO BE HUMAN?

Most of life is a fluke. It's not nearly as rational, as strategized, as planned as we love to think it is. As John Lennon was fond of saying, "Life is what happens while you are making other plans." I like to say that my life is what happened to me while I was on my way to somewhere else.

The problem is that we insist on trying to impose form and shape, plan and design on everything we do. Just letting things happen is not a comfortable skill for most people. Control is what we want. Certainty is what we like.

But there is a place in the soul for learning to leap. There is a particular virtue to darkness, to just allowing things to happen rather than wrenching them to our own specifications, for being willing to do things differently for a change, for avoiding terminal caution, for simply falling into the arms of God for a day or two instead of having to run the universe all by ourselves.

Being able to take life as it comes, to enjoy a change of plans, to break the routine, to try different things, to break out of the rut we put ourselves in so we can become the rest of ourselves, "to build our wings on the way down" is the spice that's missing in a routinized world.

THE MONASTIC WAY

There are two life lessons that take some people the greater part of a lifetime to learn. The first demands that I discover who I am—what I, myself, really want in life and what I need to give in life if I am ever to be whole. The second lies in giving myself permission to be myself no matter who tries to persuade me to be otherwise.

HOW SHALL WE LIVE?

It is interesting how we search for joy and despise suffering. Yet, suffering is a natural part of life with much to teach us and much to give us. Suffering gives us freedom and new opportunities. Joy gives us respite on the long road of life and an appreciation for heart-stopping beauty in the midst of the mundane. Most important of all, however, is the fact that suffering and joy come from the same place. Whatever is giving you your greatest happiness right now is the only thing that can really cause you great pain. Whatever is causing your suffering right now is the place beyond which you must now move in order to be able to live life joyfully again. Suffering and joy move us from end point to end point in life. They are the finger of God beckoning us to grow beyond where we are right now so that new and wonderful things can happen to us again, still, yet.

THE PSALMS

When poets talk about the human soul, they do not talk about reason, they talk about feeling. The totally human being, they enable us to see, is the one who weeps over evil, revels in goodness, loves outrageously and carries the pain of the world in healing hands. Feeling is the mark of saints. It is Vincent de Paul tending the poor on the back streets of France. Mother Teresa with a dying beggar in her arms. Florence Nightingale tending the wounded in the midst of battle. John the Apostle resting trustingly on the breast of Jesus. Damian binding the running sores of lepers on the island of Molokai, the soup kitchen people in our own towns giving hours of their lives, week after week, to feed the undernourished. Feeling, we know deep within us, signals the real measure of a soul.

HEART OF FLESH

One of the most demanding, but often overlooked, dimensions of the creation story is that when creation was finished, it wasn't really finished at all. Instead, God committed the rest of the process to us. What humans do on this earth either continues creation or obstructs it. It all depends on the way we look at life, the way we see our role in the ongoing creation of the world.

Work is our contribution to creation. It relates us to the rest of the world. It fulfills our responsibility to the future. God left us a world intact, a world with enough for everyone. The contemplative question of the time is what kind of world are we leaving to those who come after us? The contemplative sets out to shape the world in the image of God. Order, cleanliness, care of the environment bring the glory of God into the stuff of the moment, the character of the little piece of the planet for which we are responsible.

The ideal state, the contemplative knows, is not to avoid work. The first thing Genesis requires of Adam and Eve is that they "till the garden and keep it." They are, then, commanded to work long before they sin. Work is not, in Judeo-Christian tradition, punishment for sin. Work is the mark of the conscientiously human. We do not live to outgrow work. We live to work well, to work with purpose, to work with honesty and quality and artistry. The floors the contemplative mops have never been better mopped. The potatoes the contemplative grows do not damage the soil they grow in under the pretense of developing it. The machines a contemplative designs and builds are not created to destroy life but to make it more possible for everyone. The people the contemplative serves get all the care that God has given us.

The contemplative is overcome by the notion of tilling the garden and keeping it. Work does not distract us from God. It brings the reign of God closer than it was before we came. Work doesn't take us away from God. It continues the work of God through us. Work is the priesthood of the human race. It turns the ordinary into the grandeur of God.

ILLUMINATED LIFE

Remember that life is to be lived—all of it, in all of its layers and longings. Only then will we ever know our own strength and depth of soul.

THE MONASTIC WAY

We need to stop and thank God—consciously—for the good things of the day. We spend so much time wanting things to be better that we fail to see our real gifts. There are banquets in our life and we don't enjoy them because we are always grasping for something more: the perfect schedule, the perfect work, the perfect friend, the perfect community. We have to realize that God's gifts are all around us, that joy is an attitude of mind, an awareness that my life is basically good. Dissatisfaction is too often a sign of something wrong in me.

25 WINDOWS INTO THE SOUL

Longing, you see, is part of life. The only question is, what do you long for? Don't be glib about the answer. Look down deep inside yourself. What is lacking when you feel empty? What are you really thinking about when you're supposed to be thinking about something else? That's what you're longing for. Find it. It's the key to your problems in the present and the energy you have for the future.

Nobody is ever completely happy, completely satisfied. That's not because we're failures. That's because we're built that way. We're supposed to want more—or why would we ever want God enough to go through life with a restless eye, watching. Be grateful for your longings. They are what take us to the next step in life and there are many to be walked before we're whole, before we're finally home.

Someplace along the way in life we all need to learn to long for God, for what really counts. The hard thing, the good thing, is that life itself will teach us that.

THE PSALMS

A loss of commitment to beauty may be the clearest sign we have that we have lost our way to God. Without beauty we miss the glory of the face of God in the here and now.

Beauty is the most provocative promise we have of the Beautiful. It lures us and calls us and leads us on.

Souls thirst for beauty and thrive on it and by it nourish hope. It is Beauty that magnetizes the contemplative and it is the duty of the contemplative to give beauty away so that the rest of the world may, in the midst of squalor, ugliness and pain, remember that beauty is possible.

What we do not nourish within ourselves cannot exist in the world around us because we are its microcosm. We cannot moan the loss of quality in our world and not ourselves seed the beautiful in our wake. We cannot decry the loss of the spiritual and continue ourselves to function only on the level of the vulgar. We cannot hope for fullness of life without nurturing fullness of soul. We must seek beauty, study beauty, surround ourselves with beauty.

To be contemplative we must remove the clutter from our lives, surround ourselves with beauty and consciously, relentlessly, persistently, give it away until the tiny world for which we ourselves are responsible begins to reflect the raw beauty that is God.

ILLUMINATED LIFE

Beauty does not stand alone in the universe, isolated and remote, under glass and precious for its rarity. Beauty is the bridge to justice. It's the lost beauty of nature that warns us against pollution. It's the beauty in a child's face that brings us to see the ugliness of racism. It's the beauty of life that brings us to rage against the injustice that obstructs it for anyone. Beauty is the glue that holds the world together.

To bring peace, to nurture hope, to wage justice, then, it is necessary to teach beauty or nothing is too valuable to be destroyed. We may well be spending far too much time teaching skills and productivity and efficiency and far too little time on music and art and poetry and flowers and literary appreciation. To raise a child well, we must seed a place in their souls for beauty. To live life fully, we must learn to take time out for beauty.

"BEAUTY BRIDGE TO JUSTICE"
BENETVISION 2000 CALENDAR

"*Two are better* than one," the Book of Ecclesiastes teaches, "for if they fall, the one will lift the other up; but woe to the one that is alone."

It's a simple statement, a profound one, this biblical commonplace. But the conventional wisdom of a highly mobile, basically anonymous, totally fragmented society affects at least to ignore it. "No one is indispensable," we say so flippantly, so unfeelingly in a massified culture. But the words grate like sandpaper on the soul of the wizened and the loving.

There is indeed one thing that renders all of us, any of us, indispensable. As long as there is someone, somewhere whose life breathes in time with my own, I know down deep that I am indeed needed, that I have no right to die. I know that I am truly indispensable, irreplaceable, vital to a life beyond my own. To that person I am indispensable. Whatever my own needs, the love of the other has greater claim on me than I do on myself. Our friends depend on us.

To have a friend is to acknowledge that some part of someone else's life which we have held tenderly, trustingly in our own hands might well die with us. Where does grief for the dead come from, in fact, if not from the anger and sense of abandonment that emerges from the realization that some part of ourselves has been taken away from us without our permission? Grief is simply a measure of the joy, the depth that comes from growing to know another and letting them know me in ways in which I am exposed to no one else.

Indeed, to lose a friend is to be cast back into the insularism that is the self. It is a dark and sniveling place to be. It is a dangerous place to be, narrow and confined by the limits of the self. Only friendship can really save us from our own smallness.

THE FRIENDSHIP OF WOMEN

"*Do not brood* over your past mistakes and failures," the India Swami Sivananda wrote, "as this will only fill your mind with grief, regret and depression."

Regret claims to be insight. But how can it be spiritual insight to deny the good of what has been for the sake of what was not? No, regret is not insight. It is, in fact, the sand trap of the soul. It fails to understand that there are many ways to fullness of life, all of them different, all of them unique.

Regret is a temptation. It entices us to lust for what never was in the past rather than to bring new energy to our changing present. It is a misuse of the aging process. One of the functions—one of the gifts—of aging is to become comfortable with the self we are, rather than to mourn what we are not. When we devalue it, we bring everything we are and were into question, into doubt. We doubt the God who made us and walks with us all the way to the end.

THE GIFT OF YEARS

The isolation that marks any serious struggle is a call to recognize that life is full of gifts that come and go, come and go as we ourselves come and go through the many stages of life. Detachment from the idea that there is only one way for me to go through life joyfully is its key. The pain of loss is a real and a present thing. It manacles my soul and breaks my heart, yes. But holy indifference—detachment—teaches me that there is no room for isolation, abandonment, death of the spirit when I lose one thing because I know that there is something else waiting for me in its place. If only I can allow myself to watch for it, to wait for it, to grasp it when it comes.

But the truth remains: Nothing lasts. No single thing can consume our entire life's meaning. No single thing can give us total satisfaction. Nothing is worth everything: neither past, nor present nor future. It isn't true that the loss of any single thing will destroy us. Everything in life has some value and life is full of valuable things, things worth living for, things worth doing, things worth becoming, things worth loving again. It is only a matter of being detached enough from one thing to be open to everything else.

The essence of life is not to find the one thing that satisfies us but to realize that nothing can ever completely satisfy us.

SCARRED BY STRUGGLE, TRANSFORMED BY HOPE

The great spiritual question, then, becomes what to do when change comes demanding courage and finds us shivering in the cubbyhole of our souls, sure that life changed is life ended. The answer may, in the end, depend less on raw risk and more on the realization that change is a quality of growth. Real risk is not motion for its own sake. "To live is to change," Newman wrote, "and to be perfect is to have changed often." Real risk is a gamble on the unfinished self, then, on what God gave us to begin with but has only now required of us in full.

Change points are those moments in life at which we get inside ourselves to find that we are not, at the end, really one person at all. We are many—each of them lying in wait to come to life. We are each a composite of experiences and abilities, of possibilities and hopes, of memories and wonder, of gifts and dreams. Every stage of life calls on a different dimension of the self. Every stage of life is another grace of being that teaches us something new about ourselves, that demands something sterner of ourselves, that enables us to learn something deeper about our God. At one stage of life, we rely on personality; at another on our skill; at a third on a latent love of adventure; at others on imagination; at others on faith.

Change may frighten us, of course, but it may just as surely free us from our old selves and freshen us for life newborn. Change dusts off our dreams and explodes us into new beginnings.

THE STORY OF RUTH

Try saying this silently to everyone and everything you see for thirty days and see what happens to your own soul: *I wish you happiness now and whatever will bring happiness to you in the future.* If we said it to the sky, we would have to stop polluting. If we said it when we see the ponds and lakes and streams, we would have to stop using them as garbage dumps and sewers. If we said it to small children, we would have to stop abusing them, even in the name of training. If we said it to people, we would have to stop stoking the fires of enmity around us. Beauty and human warmth would take root in us like a clear, hot June day. We would change.

IN A HIGH SPIRITUAL SEASON

Opposite: In 2006, Joan Chittister visited
an Iraqi refugee camp in Syria as part of
Global Peace Initiative of Women, a partner
organization of the United Nations.
Photograph by Janelle Surpris.
Courtesy Benetvision.

CHAPTER 3

ᴡHO IS A CONTEMPLATIVE?

Contemplatives are not fakirs, gurus or professional religious types. "Contemplative" and "cloister" are not synonyms. Cloister is at best only one of many vehicles to contemplation, needed by some, irrelevant to others who see the face of another Jesus in the poor, the rejected, the starving, the beaten, and love it dearly. To call only one of these "the contemplative life" is to overlook entirely the contemplative dimension of all life—the life of the mother who feels the presence of God while bathing her baby, the life of the man who feels God's breaking heart in his own when he sees young soldiers walk by, the lives of old people who have spent all their lives doing good so that the reign of God could finally come, the lives of young people who offer themselves up for the love of another on altars of their own.

Contemplation has to do with seeing life as it is, not with escaping one to find another. Contemplatives are ordinary people who are extraordinarily conscious of the impelling life of God both within them and around them. They live under the impulse of the God who made them and listen to the small, deep voice within that guides them from the crucifix of Christ to concern for the vastness of a creation not made for them alone. The contemplative sees the meaning of eternity in every moment in time.

IN SEARCH OF BELIEF

Humility and contemplation are the invisible twins of the spiritual life. One without the other is impossible. In the first place, there is no such thing as a contemplative life without the humility that takes us beyond the myth of our own grandeur to the cosmic grandeur of God. In the second, once we really know the grandeur of God we get the rest of life—ourselves included—in perspective.

ILLUMINATED LIFE

Early in my monastic life, I remember working very hard at prayer. I prepared and prepared for prayer. At that time, our prayer was in Latin. While I wasn't all that bad in Latin, no one really wrestles with the nuances of the spiritual life in another language let alone a dead one. So, I prepared in English as well. Yet, even though my preparation improved, I couldn't see that anything was happening in my life. I didn't feel closer to God or more aware of God's presence.

Then in the early 1960s, I was given a copy of *Abandonment to Divine Providence* by Jean-Pierre de Caussade. He added an element that had been missing for me. It was the concept of the sacrament of the present moment, the notion that what is <u>now</u> is where God is for me now.

The awareness of God's presence had become my greatest value. After that, I began to see that we are steeped in God. But our awareness of this is so limited. I think that's true because we have been trained to pray, instead of being trained in prayer.

PRAYING MAGAZINE, JAN/FEB 1991
INTERVIEW WITH ART WINTER

God is radiant light, blazing fire, asexual spirit, colorless wind. God is the magnet of our souls, the breath of our hearts, the stuff of our lives. God is no one's pigment, no one's flag and no one's gender. And those who certify their God under any of those credentials make a new idol in the desert. To be enlightened we must let God speak to us through everything—and everyone—through whom God shines in life.

IN THE HEART OF THE TEMPLE

It is always spiritual questions that undergird the life issues in which we find ourselves. Marriage, business, children, professions are all defined as if contemplation did not need to be a natural part of them. But no one needs contemplation more than the harried mother, the irritable father, the ambitious executive, the striving professional, the poor woman, the sick man. Then, in those situations, we need reflection, understanding, meaning, peace of soul more than ever. Contemplation is the missing quality of the beleaguered life.

LIVING IN THE BREATH OF THE SPIRIT

Contemplation is not for its own sake. To live a contemplative life, to be spiritual, does not mean that we spend life in some kind of sacred spa designed to save us from having to deal with the down and dirty parts of life. The contemplative life is not spiritual escapism. Contemplation is immersion in the God who created the world for all of us.

RADICAL GRACE NEWSPAPER, APRIL/MAY/JUNE 2006

The Desert Mothers and Fathers said that contemplation was best accomplished through manual labor. The ancient literature tells lots of stories about the work that was done by contemplatives—basket weaving, for example, is frequently mentioned.

The link between work and contemplation is very interesting. The Desert Fathers and Mothers were saying contemplation is not idleness. Further, it's not concentration on something else. So, who is better for the contemplative life than the person who is working, but who is not totally caught up in the things he or she is working with? For a person with this approach, work or being busy can become a contemplative act, can be the occasion for fostering the awareness of God's presence.

Many people, I think, sense this. They seem to know intuitively that growing a garden, or painting a house, or raking the leaves are good things to do. Good things happen to people when they are doing such tasks. They use them as a vehicle for bringing their lives to wholeness. That's contemplative. That's coming to awareness. That's giving yourself a chance to see yourself as you are.

PRAYING MAGAZINE JAN/FEB 1991
INTERVIEW WITH ART WINTER

God is indeed everywhere—in the darkness as well as in light, in the ordinary life lived with extraordinary consciousness, in the sacred center of a creation that is secular to its marrow. It is in the separation of life into categories of the holy and the unholy, the spiritual and the material, the earthly and the heavenly that the human soul gets divided as well.

LIVING IN THE BREATH OF THE SPIRIT

The flight from Manila to Tokyo had been, to all appearances, totally routine. We were about an hour from touchdown when the captain came on the intercom: "When we left Manila," the voice said, "we got a signal from the on-board computer telling us that there is something wrong with the plane's landing gear. We have no idea what that is or how serious it may be. Your cabin crew will instruct you how to prepare for a crash landing. Emergency vehicles will meet us on the runway. Please listen carefully now to your flight attendant..." The school boy next to me said, "How do I tell them to call my sister first? I don't want my mother to hear about this on a phone." Then, the noise in the cabin stopped. The entire planeload of tourists and business people, of whole families and solitary travelers like me went dead, cold, silent. For almost an hour we packed up our gear, removed glasses and shoes and jewelry. Then, we simply sat and waited, frozen in silence. "Did you say a prayer?" someone asked me later when I was telling the story. "No, I didn't say a prayer; I became a prayer."

THE MONASTIC WAY

If there is a temptation in the Christian life, it is probably contemplation. Physicians talk to us about "stress"; psychologists talk to us about "burnout"; sociologists talk to us about achieving "space"; educators talk to us about reflection and "process." And we all come lusting for a cave to crawl into to do it, or at least a little cottage on a hill overlooking the water, or even a small log cabin in the woods. Any place as long as it's someplace appropriate; some place not here; some place simple but comfortable, of course. A place for my books, my typewriter, my tape recorder. Just me and my God. Or is it me and the gods I've made?

If there is a sin in the Christian life it is probably action. We talk about "strategizing" and "mobilizing" and "lobbying" and "renewing" and "aligning" and "reforming" as if it were all up to structures; as if action were enough. We do and do and do. And there's the problem. We set out to *do* something that the world needs, instead of to *be* something that the world needs. We set out to change instead of to illuminate. And we wonder why, with all the changes, nothing ever changes. After all the changes come, there is still the fighting, still the poverty, still the greed, still the exploitation.

Why? Because deep down inside where it counts, there is still the anger, still the arrogance, still the attitudes of control. Except that now I'm the one in control. The Chinese wrote: "Now people exploit people but after the revolution it will be just the opposite."

The contemplative questions for people of action in our day are: Who will *be* and also *do*? How can we do and also be? The problem of this culture is that we make natural enemies out of prayer and transforming action when the two are really Siamese twins: either without the other is incomplete.

PAX CHRISTI USA MAGAZINE, JUNE 1985

The contemplative realizes that everything in life has for its purpose the kindling of the God-life within us. And so the contemplative goes on with joy and resounds with praise and lives in gratitude. Always. What better way to bring the light of the diamond to glow in darkness.

ILLUMINATED LIFE

There are books aplenty written on the subject of prayer, of course, but I have come to the point where I doubt that anybody can really "teach" anybody how to pray. That, I figure, is what life does. We can learn prayer forms, of course, but we do not learn either the function or the purpose of prayer until life drags us to it, naked and in pain.

THE MONASTIC WAY

The function of prayer is certainly not to cajole God into saving us from ourselves. "Please, God, don't let us die in nuclear war" surely is not real prayer. We can stop nuclear war ourselves by stopping the manufacture of nuclear weapons. Humans created them and humans can destroy them. No, the function of prayer is not magic. The function of prayer is not the bribery of the Infinite. The function of prayer is not to change the mind of God about decisions we have already made for ourselves.

The function of prayer is to change my own mind, to put on the mind of Christ, to enable grace to break into me.

WISDOM DISTILLED FROM THE DAILY

When we have prayed prayers long enough, all the words drop away and we begin to live in the presence of God. Then prayer is finally real.

When we find ourselves sinking into the world around us with a sense of purpose, an inner light and deep and total trust that whatever happens is right for us, then we have become prayer.

When we kneel down, we admit the magnitude of God in the universe and our own smallness in the face of it. When we stand with hands raised, we recognize the presence of God in life and our own inner glory because of it.

All life is in the hands of God. Even the desire to pray is the grace to pray. The movement to pray is the movement of God in our souls. Our ability to pray depends on the power and place of God in our life. We pray because God attracts us and we pray only because God is attracting us. We are not, in other words, even the author of our own prayer life. It is the goodness of God, not any virtue that we have developed on our own, that brings us to the heart of God. And it is with God's help that we seek to go there.

THE MONASTIC WAY

"Never pray in a room without windows," the Talmud teaches. Never pray, in other words, without keeping one eye on the world around you. Never pray

to escape the world. Pray only to have the courage, the commitment, the piety to take it in.

PASTORAL MUSIC MAGAZINE, OCTOBER 1995

Some people ask, "How are we supposed to pray?" Other people ask—more correctly, I think—"How do *you* pray?" Prayer, you see, is a very personal part of spiritual development. It changes as we change. It deepens as we grow. It simplifies as we do as the years go by.

Prayer centers us and stretches us and lays us bare, as the prayer says, "of all our self-conceits." Inside ourselves, we know who we are and what we need and what we lack and what we don't understand and what we long for as we go. It is this awareness and the dependence on God it brings with it that are the wellspring of prayer.

Prayer is the awareness that it is not a question of whether or not God is present to us—that we can take for granted; instead prayer is process of *our* becoming present to God.

So, real prayer can be fed by any one of a number of things—scripture, nature, personal experience, emotional pressures, intellectual commitment to the God who is greater than any idea of God we can possibly have. But whatever the life-link that brings us into consciousness of God, in the end, the way we each pray has something to do with who we are.

The whole notion, then, that there is some prayer formula or ritual or schedule or style that is right for everyone is, at best, naive. Even the *Rule of Benedict*, that sixth-century document on the spiritual life that devotes more chapters to prayer than to any other topic in the *Rule*, ends the long outline of psalms and readings by saying, "But if any of the monastics know a better way, let them arrange them differently." No single form, we find, is the ultimate valuation of a life of prayer. And in another place Benedict says, "Let prayer be short and pure unless, perhaps, it is lengthened by divine grace." The purpose of choral prayer, it is clear, is simply to inspire personal prayer.

PRAYING WITH THE BENEDICTINES
FOREWORD

To be a contemplative it is necessary to walk through nature softly, to be in tune with the rhythm of life, to learn from the cycles of time, to listen to the heartbeat of the universe, to love nature, to protect nature, and to discover in nature the presence and the power of God. To be a contemplative it is necessary to grow a plant, love an animal, walk in the rain, and profess our consciousness of God into a lifetime of pulsating seasons.

ILLUMINATED LIFE

Contemplative prayer is prayer that leads us to see our world through the eyes of God. It unstops our ears to hear the poverty of widows, the loneliness of widowers, the cry of women, the vulnerability of children, the struggle of outcasts, the humanity of enemies, the insights of the uneducated, the tensions of bureaucrats, the fears of rulers, the wisdom of the holy, the power of the powerless.

WISDOM DISTILLED FROM THE DAILY

The person with the enlightened heart knows that the purpose of the human voice is to give sound to the voiceless until, finally, the world begins to hear what the enlightened heart has come to know—God's presence here, now, in everyone.

IN THE HEART OF THE TEMPLE

It isn't so much that people leave religion, I think, as it is that like Olympic runners on a mission, they come to a moment in life when they go on beyond the system to the very source of the light. It is the plight of the mystic to enter the universe of God alone where no charts or maps or signs exist to guide us and assure us of the way. It is a serious and disturbing moment, one after which we are never quite the same.

CALLED TO QUESTION

In the end, the fruit of contemplation is joy. When we walk with God, what is there to fear? Serenity comes to those who walk with God. Surety comes to those who see God in everything. Peace comes to those who know that what is, is of God, if only we will make it so.

ILLUMINATED LIFE

Opposite: Joan Chittister and children from Hwacheon, South Korea, at a Peace Park dedication during a meeting of the International Peace Council. Photo by Madeline Yu, OSB. Courtesy Benetvision.

CHAPTER 4

WHERE CAN
WE FIND HOPE?

"Hope," the fantasy writer Margaret Weis wrote, "is the denial of reality."

I completely disagree.

Reality is the only thing we have that can possibly nourish hope. Hope is not based on the ability to fabricate a better future; it is grounded in the ability to remember with new understanding an equally difficult past—either our own or someone else's. The fact is that our memories are the seedbed of our hope. They are the only things we have that prove to us that whatever it was we ever before thought would crush us to the grave, would trample our spirits into perpetual dust, would fell us in our tracks, had actually been survived. And if that is true, then whatever we are wrestling with now can also be surmounted.

Hope is not some kind of delusional optimism to be resorted to because we simply cannot face the hard facts that threaten to swamp our hearts. People do die and leave us. Friends do leave and desert us. Businesses do crumble and destroy us financially. Loves do dry up and disappear. Desires do come to dust. Careers do come to ruin. Disease does debilitate us. Evil does exist. But through it all, hope remains, nevertheless, a choice.

Scarred by Struggle, Transformed by Hope

Confidence and hope are different things. Confidence is the inner conviction that we are equal to whatever task is before us. It is the certainty that we are bright enough, strong enough, powerful enough to meet a challenge and best it.

Hope, on the other hand, is what sustains us when we have little or no confidence left. At the end of a bad stretch, hope—hope that the will of God will finally prevail—is all that is left to sustain us. When it becomes clear that the things on which we have depended aren't really dependable, hope must replace confidence, or nothing can replace confidence at all.

Hope knows that whatever happens, God lives. Hope expects that however bad it looks, this moment will ultimately yield something good. Hope says begin again.

Winners may have confidence, but real heroes—those who have seen bad times and lived to rise above them—live in hope.

Beliefnet.org
December 20, 2000

Hope is rooted in the past but believes in the future. God's world is in God's hands, hope says, and therefore cannot possibly be hopeless. Life, already fulfilled in God, is only the process of coming to realize that we have been given everything we need to come to fullness of life, both here and hereafter. The greater the hope, the greater the appreciation of life now, the greater the confidence in the future, whatever it is.

But if struggle is the process of evolution from

spiritual emptiness to spiritual wisdom, hope is a process as well. Hope, the response of the spiritual person to struggle, takes us from the risk of inner stagnation, of emotional despair, to a total transformation of life. Every stage of the process of struggle is a call to move from spiritual torpor to spiritual vitality. It is an invitation to live at an antipodal depth of soul, a higher level of meaning than the ordinary, the commonplace generally inspires. The spirituality of struggle gives birth to the spirituality of hope.

SCARRED BY STRUGGLE, TRANSFORMED BY HOPE

The first spring flower you see say to yourself over and over again: Hope rages, hope rages, hope rages in this world. Then ask yourself: And what am I doing to make it real?

THE PSALMS

Everyone is struck down by something in life. It is the detour that determines the definition of the journey. We can lose our way then and there, stay stuck in unfamiliar territory, stall and give up. Or we can take the new direction confident that in the end we will end up exactly where we were meant to be whether we can see how that is possible right now or not.

LIVING WELL

The mystics also taught that this dark night was a necessary moment in the development of the soul. Sure of the absence of God, we actually become aware of the presence of God. It is the paradox of faith. It is the fortunate misadventure of life. By losing everything, we come to the realization that everything is far less than we think it is and far more than we ever dreamed it could be. In the end, everything is what cannot be taken away, what cannot be lost, what will not fail us in our hope. Everything is the nagging awareness that always there is more and that always I have it. I am reduced by misery to stop and look through the darkness to the light on the horizon that never changes. Darkness becomes the incubator of light.

SCARRED BY STRUGGLE, TRANSFORMED BY HOPE

Endurance shines as the hallmark of the prophets, the lodestar of the prophetic. As much as normalcy marks the prophet as sensible, and compassion marks the prophet as human, endurance tests the truth of the witness, the meaning and the merit of the testimony itself.

Those who are willing to practice endurance when it appears insane, when it has no hope of prevailing, and when it consumes everything else in its path are those who know a greater truth, a more promising hope, a truer way to wholeness than the world around them has to offer. That kind of endurance is of God. It transcends human concerns and commands human attention. That kind of endurance holds on to the divine in life, even when life itself gives in to making gods of gold in deserts of sand. Prophetic endurance holds on, cries out, speaks up, stands firm, whatever the pressure, however long the time, until, whether or not they agree, people listen and think.

LIGUORIAN MAGAZINE, APRIL 1995

"*If you* expect to see the final results of your work," an Arab proverb teaches, "you have simply not asked a big enough question." To sustain a stay in a dry and barren desert, it is necessary to be about something great enough to be worth a lifetime of unrewarded effort.

There are simply some divine cravings in life—the liberation of the poor, the equality of women, the humanity of the entire human race—that are worth striving for, living for, dying for, finished or unfinished, for as long as it takes to achieve them.

COMPASS MAGAZINE, MAY/JUNE 1992

It is so easy to make God to our own image and likeness. It is so easy to get stuck into the images we make of the Unimaginable. It is so easy to make God small and call that faith.

The evidence in every sector of human life makes the point only too well: open-mindedness, breadth of vision, the universal mind rise all too rare. The real sin of Eden, surely, was the rupture of relationships between the people themselves and the people and God. Redemption, then, must certainly depend on our healing our relationships, not on our cementing their tensions.

Given the loss of past absolutes and the shift in the social consensus on national values—both of which are inevitable in the wake of technological development, major cultural transformations and new social realities—people cling to old certainties like shipwreck survivors to lifeboats.

What we want then is stability, what we fear is loss of control, what we get are new questions for which there are no ready answers. It is times such as these that plumb the human spirit to its depths and demand more than pettiness and paltry answers to cosmic questions. But do we dare ask such questions? Do we dare to confront an old faith with new realities?

In times like those, people do one of two things: either they attempt to retreat into the past or they lose all respect for the slow-moving institutional present. They become either reactionary or anarchic. They are drawn like magnets to one extreme or the other.

The problem is, of course, that in times of great social dislocation, the need for personal security outweighs the challenge of faith and the call to new understandings. Full of anxiety at what may be lost and at what will befall us if it is, we fail to give spiritual and intellectual space to newer and broader insights.

Fear reigns. We set out to protect ourselves and, in the process, often destroy those around us.

Due to fear and lack of faith, we lose vision and courage. We deny both the questions and the possibilities of new answers. We suppress anything and anyone who raises new questions. We panic.

It is precisely in times like these that a world in flux needs a prophetic commitment to principle in the face of practices that have long since gone awry or that beg to be reviewed. What the world needs then is openness to the Holy Spirit and a commitment to basic tenets of truth and justice and goodness and to the will of God for all humankind. We need a faith than can function in the present, not a religion that mirrors the past.

It is not an easy to achieve, this openness to the Spirit. It demands that we let go of our own ideas to make way for new manifestations of the presence of God in our time. It is not a comfortable call, this invitation from God to walk unknowingly toward a distant future, but it is the ultimate manifestation of response to the Spirit.

We like to separate the prophets of the Church from the people of the Church. We like to separate ourselves from the demands of greatness. But the prophetic dimension of the Church—as Scripture demonstrates in the prophetic figures of Amos, Hosea, Micah, Isaiah and Ezekiel—is realized in simple souls just like us— ordinary citizens, compassionate lovers, justice-seeking and persistent idealists who move with courage into places that everyone else takes for granted, and speak God's word—loudly, clearly, boldly—in the midst of human chaos, whatever levy it imposes on their own lives.

Prophecy, in other words, is not a luxury; it is an essential dimension of the Christian life. We will not be forgiven our disdain of holy risk in the name of weakness.

LIGUORIAN MAGAZINE, NOVEMBER 1995

I would argue, my friends, that we do not have a crisis of Christianity. We have a crisis of significance, a crisis of spirituality, which leads us to a crisis of contemporary credibility, of institutional structure called "Church," and of the prophetic proclamation of hope.

Augustine says that of the three theological virtues of faith, hope and love, hope is greatest. He writes, "Faith only tells us that God is real, and love only tells us that God is love, but hope tells us that God will work God's will." Then in the next paragraph Augustine writes, "Hope has two loving daughters, anger and courage—anger, so that what must not be cannot be, and courage, so that what must be may be."

My prayer for the leaders of the Church and its ministers is that we will lead with a touch of anger and a burst of courage.

THE JOURNAL OF THE CATHOLIC WOMEN'S NETWORK, AUGUST 1993

Rebuilders are artists of the soul who shape a piece of human creation and leave the results to the kiln of time. They do not claim to have all the answers. They claim to honor the questions. They are prepared to float forever, if necessary, to find a better world, to shape a finer piece of the planet…. The soul of a rebuilder is based on the ability to look lovingly into nothingness and know that there is something there worth going to, worth giving this life to doing so that the lives of those that follow can be better still.

THERE IS A SEASON

Leadership is the ability to see the vision beyond the reality and to make a road where no road has been. Spiritual leadership is the ability to question the present in order to show the way to the greater good, whether it is popular to pursue that good or not. The questions of leadership are organizational ones of course, but they are spiritual ones, too. They have something to do with the structures of a society, yes, but they have more to do with the spirit of that society and the compass of its soul. Spiritual leadership is, as the psalmist says, the ability "to be a light in the darkness for the upright." And it is often a lonely, lonely task. Knowing when to go is one thing; breaking the path to it is another.

IGNATIUS LOYOLA: SPIRIT & PRACTICE FOR TODAY

Prophets read hearts, not cards or crystal balls or configurations in the heavens. What is in the human heart they compare to what is in the mind of God. The contrast becomes prophecy.

LIGUORIAN MAGAZINE, APRIL 1995

Winston Churchill wrote once, "I would rather fail in a cause which I know must some day triumph than triumph in a cause that I know must some day fail." In a Church where the ideals are so clear and the implementation is so slow, this is a particularly important reflection.

The Zen master taught us, "The seed never sees the flower." In a world where everything is changing and nothing ever seems to get resolved, in a Church where revelation comes an inch at a time, the notion of slow growth is comforting.

The philosopher said, "If I knew that the world would end tomorrow, I would plant an apple tree today." In a world where whole classes of people are oppressed and decisions are justified on the basis of authority alone or on the basis of a tradition that is more manufactured than revelatory, the idea of never allowing the destructiveness of the present to defeat our commitment to achieve the ideal is essential.

Vision, sacrifice and hope are the caretakers of the future. Without them tomorrow is impossible and today is straw.

COMPASS MAGAZINE, MAY/JUNE 1992

Vision is not the ability to predict the future; it is a commitment to pursue possibility. Vision asks questions no one else even seems to know exist. Vision is the grace to evaluate the present and then to ask, Why not? of the future.

SEEING WITH OUR SOULS

Opposite: Joan Chittister and the Dalai Lama at the first Emory Summit on Religion, Conflict and Peacemaking at Emory University, Atlanta, GA, 2007. Photograph by Myron McGhee. Courtesy Benetvision.

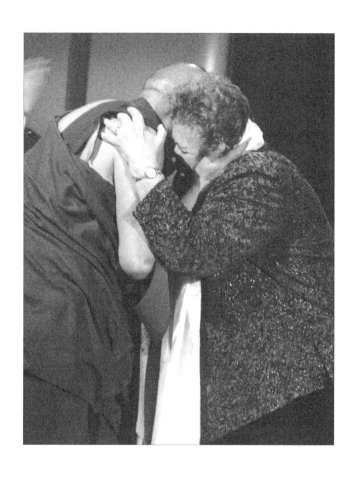

CHAPTER 5

HOW CAN WE
LIVE IN PEACE?

In 1995 I become a founding member of the International Committee for the Peace Council, a body of high profile religious figures from every major spiritual tradition in the world: Hindu, Buddhist, Jewish, Muslim and Christian. For a professed representative of the Catholic "ghetto," the first meeting was a shocking collection of Asian monks, Hindu swamis, Muslim imams, Catholic monastics and a Nobel Peace Prize Bishop, Protestant pastors and religious scholars from every tradition. What can possibly be accomplished here?

One of the Peace Councilors is Maha Ghosananda. A small round man with round eyes and round head and round body, a veritable circle of orange sunburst, he smiles a glowing smile across the table. But he never says a thing. He just sits there in his orange robes cross-legged on the chair, looking seraphic, serene, very comfortable and very out of place at the same time. He is some kind of living icon of peace, I'm sure, but just what I don't know.

All day he smiles and smiles as we discuss going, as a sign of religious unity, to places where religion is at the root of conflict: to Chiapas, to Belfast, to Jerusalem, to India. I begin to wonder what he possibly knows about all of this, if anything. When he's out of the room, we're told that this is the Supreme Buddhist Patriarch of Cambodia. This is the monk who has begun the dharma walks across the country to call attention to the minefields there that have crippled so many and killed even more.

Then, out of nowhere it happens. The reason he does it, they say, is because his family—his entire family: brothers and sisters, nieces and nephews, in-laws and distant cousins were murdered in the Pol Pot Regime. He has no one left in the world. No one at all. So he does it, because as a Buddhist, he must teach peace.

What can we learn from the spiritual heritage of other traditions? Answer: that God is in the heart of humankind and if we listen clearly, we can hear that same voice in another language. We can hear the voice in the Koran, the Dhammapada, the Bhagavad Gita, the Talmud and the Lotus Sermons. All we have to do is listen.

THE MONASTIC WAY

The one continuing thread from earliest time until now in the Benedictine tradition is the tradition of peace-making. We know historically that early Christians did not participate in the military. And though historians struggle with whether the major concern was that they could not participate in the emperor worship common to soldiers in the Roman Empire or whether the primary concern was that Christians do not kill, the fact remains that the data reflects unquestionably that the early Christians simply believed "Love one another" and "Thou shalt not kill" were absolute mandates.

That pacifist tradition is still honored by governments. We don't draft monks, priests, or clerics, because we recognize that from time immemorial this is a peacemaking tradition. In the Middle Ages, monks were the first groups to raise the notion of rules for modern warfare. It's the monks who first attempt to promote the peace of God, and then to promote the compromised position of the truce of God which says: If you must fight, then all we ask for is an agreement that you don't fight on Thursday, because Thursday is the memorial of the Ascension, and you don't fight on Friday, because Friday is the memorial of the Passion, and you don't fight on Saturday, because Saturday is the memorial of the Entombment, and, of course, you can't fight on Sunday, because Sunday is the memorial of the Resurrection.

It was medieval monasteries and monks who tried to control this open season on human beings.

Now if you're Benedictine and the most ancient motto of the order is "Pax," and you live in the 20th century where you are now capable of replicating 1,600,000 Hiroshimas, then surely there is some special obligation on the part of the Benedictine to address that continuing issue.

SOJOURNERS MAGAZINE
AUG/SEPT 1987
INTERVIEW WITH EDITORS

"Violence in a house," the rabbis say, "is like a worm in fruit." It destroys what otherwise looks healthy and firm and good but which is harboring within it the cause of its own decline. Violence is eating the heart right out of this country—in private homes and police stations, in personal relationships, playgrounds and public policies. Violence is our national disease. Walking gently through life is our only real hope of gentling the world.

IN THE HEART OF THE TEMPLE

Q. What can a peacemaker say to those people who feel powerless to do anything about the arms race?

A. A lot of folks say, "Well, I can't do anything about that. I'm just one person, and the problem's too big." Typically, ordinary citizens feel overwhelmed once they realize there's enough nuclear power in the world to blow up the globe several times over.

I saw a wonderful program on PBS titled, "The Problem of Evil." On it, one commentator talked about the death camps of World War II and asked whether the Nazi military leaders were the real culprits. Equally responsible, he maintained, were the lawyers, the bureaucrats, and the foot soldiers—the people who let the exterminations go on unchallenged. There isn't a single instance, that I can find on record, of just one soldier who refused to turn on the gas or push the last naked baby into the ovens. I'm sure they all were overwhelmed, that they said the same thing: "But there's nothing I can do..."

I find, however, that the most freeing element of a serious issue is when one person says no. If only one person just says, "No, I won't..." it makes people stop and think. It gathers people around you—kind of like the E. F. Hutton commercial. Try it at a cocktail party and see what happens! You see, as long as you make an issue discussible, then it's thinkable; and as long as it's thinkable, it's possible.

SALT MAGAZINE, MARCH 1989
INTERVIEW WITH EDITORS

The fact is that we mix the national religion and the Christian religion as a matter of course. This country, we presume, like the Jerusalemites before us, is especially favored by God, under God's singular protection, distinctly chosen to do God's will. To those types Abraham Lincoln taught in the course of the Civil War, "The question is not whether or not God is on our side. The question is whether or not we are on God's side."

THERE IS A SEASON

For war to be just, the first criteria is that it must only be waged in the face of "real and certain danger." So when did we start waging war "just in case"?

To be just, we're taught in the second criteria for a just war, war must be declared by "the competent authority." But presidents no longer declare war at all. They simply ask congress for the right to use "whatever force is necessary" to resolve an immediate problem. Or strike first and discuss it later. As Boake Carter put it, "In time of war, the first casualty is truth."

To be just, a war must pass the third criteria of the just war, the test of "comparative justice." The rights to be preserved must justify the killing that will be done in their name. So the question must be what rights do we as a people stand to lose if we don't go to war? And what rights have we lost that we must recover? Now there's a tough one.

For a war to be just, the tradition teaches, the fourth criteria is that "All peaceful alternatives must have been exhausted." Whatever happened to the days when cities weren't attacked, they were simply put under siege? Or has attack become too easy to bother engaging the soul and the mind in the task of preventing it?

The fifth condition of the just war is "right intention." It can only be fought for a "just cause," a situation that outweighs the value of the number of lives that will be lost and the amount of damage that will be done in the waging of it. And what side that attacks first can ever plead "just cause"? To do that puts a nation in the place of God the Judge, a judge that punishes us before we even sin.

The sixth criteria of the just war is "the probability of success." No one is to rush a nation or a people into organized suicide, however noble the cause. But in this age, when nuclear and biological weapons stand at the ready, is any war anything but an invitation either to slaughter or to suicide?

The final criteria of the just war are "proportionality and discrimination." The damage to be inflicted must be proportionate to the good to be achieved, and the innocent, the noncombatants, are to be spared.

To destroy a country to punish a government is at very least barbaric. Surely destruction of the quality of life for local noncombatants makes a war unjust.

In an age when defoliation, ecological disaster, water pollution, starvation and septic eruptions go on killing thousands for years after a cease-fire is finally achieved, how can any major military campaign be considered "proportional" anymore?

BECOMING FULLY HUMAN

At the first Iraqi-American dialogue convened by the Women's Global Peace Initiative in New York on March 29, the differences were plain. The women's first agenda did not concentrate on who did what or who profited or lost by the doing of it. "Take the oil. We don't care about the oil," one woman called across the room. "We never got any value from it anyway," she went on. "Never mind yesterday," another woman said in answer to the Sunni-Shi'ite tensions. "Forget who did what to whom. We must turn the page now. We must rebuild the country."

"And what is the first thing that must be done to rebuild the country?" we asked them. I sat with my hands over the keyboard, sure that the list would be long and varied. I was wrong. To a woman, the call was clear: "Take care of our children."

"FROM WHERE I STAND," NCRONLINE.ORG
APRIL 10, 2006

Who will give Catholics a theology of the unjust war that makes us focus, at the outset, on the results of war on innocent people instead of at the processes of beginning one?

Maybe it's time to look into the human heart rather than into tomes of commentaries written for another world at another time, commentaries that treat war as an abstract philosophical problem rather than a human aberration.

We Catholics do not philosophize about abortion, for instance. We simply say it's wrong. We do not philosophize about unjust wage and working conditions. We deplore them. We do not philosophize about infidelity in marriage. We condemn it.

But when it comes to brutal, total, all-out war, we find it impossible to distinguish between AK-47's and the creation of a nuclear "deterrence," between self-defense and imminent ecological disaster. And for

justification we refer to the presence of war in the Old
Testament, an argument from the past that we would
not tolerate in science or medicine or law.

SALT MAGAZINE
MAY 1992

What we destroy we defeat, true, but most of all we
destroy something in ourselves. What we do to one another gouges out the center of our own lives. To napalm
children is to pour acid on my own soul.

To bomb an innocent people, an illiterate people,
a destitute people into tent cities on foreign borders as
we did in Afghanistan, babies in their bellies and old
people on their backs, is obscene.

To turn whole city neighborhoods and towns to ash
overnight as we did in Iraq, to throw an entire country
into economic disarray, bomb out their electrical grids
and water supplies, stand by while their most ancient
treasures of world significance are looted, and to kill
civilians while claiming that we do not make war on
the innocent is a most sophisticated lie.

And then to wonder why guns become the
playthings of children, or why families are torn apart
by domestic murders, or why women are routinely
beaten, or why drugs become the desensitizer of choice
in a world where violence is social and economic and
domestic policy as well as military, is to raise denial
to the level of high art. Indeed, the blood of our own

children runs red in our streets because we have taught our children violence very well—and they have learned it quickly. We are reaping what we have sown. We are getting what we asked for.

IN THE HEART OF THE TEMPLE

It was a hot and honest session in that meeting of Palestinian and Israeli women in Oslo, Norway. The Palestinian women said that they supported the Israelis' right to an independent state; the Israeli women said that they supported the Palestinians' right to resources, political integrity and freedom to live in the land. It was a significant political moment.

Nevertheless, what happened after the conference adjourned may, in the end, prove to be even more significant.

On the last night of the assembly, one of these women went to the other and asked to continue the discussion about what had been lost and what must be gained if the two peoples are ever to live together well. They went out for coffee together. I don't know what was said. I only know that the conversation went on until after midnight.

When it came time to leave, the Israeli woman—old enough to be the Palestinian's mother—decided she would walk the young woman to her hotel. But then the young Palestinian realized how far the older woman would have to walk alone back to her own place of residence and insisted that she walk her halfway back again.

"I've had a wonderful night," the Israeli woman said as they parted. "This time with you was itself worth the conference."

The young Palestinian woman went silent for a moment. "I'm glad for you," she said, "but I'm confused."

The Israeli woman winced inside, "Why? What's wrong?" she asked.

"Oh, nothing is wrong," the younger woman said. "I'm just confused. I don't know what to do now that my enemy has become my friend."

The next day, in the Tel Aviv airport, the Israeli women whisked through customs and baggage claim. The Palestinian women did not. When the Israeli women realized that all the Palestinians had been detained, they turned around, went back and refused to leave the customs hall themselves until all the Palestinians were released.

That, I learned, is what it means to proceed in the "ways of peace." It means having the courage to make human connections with those we fear, with those we hate, with those who think differently than we do. It means refusing to leave the other behind as we go.

"FROM WHERE I STAND," NCRONLINE.ORG
JULY 8, 2003

War is a depredation of the human spirit that is sold as the loftiest of livelihoods. To hide the rape and pillage, the degradation and disaster, the training of human beings to become animals in ways we would allow no animals to be, we have concocted a language of mystification. We count casualties now in terms of "collateral damage," the number of millions of civilians we are prepared to lose in nuclear war and still call ourselves winners. We call the deadliest weapons in the history of humankind, the most benign of names: Little Boy, Bambi, Peacekeepers. The nuclear submarine used to launch Cruise missiles that can target and destroy 250 first-class cities at one time, for instance, we name "Corpus Christi," Body of Christ, a blasphemy used to describe the weapon that will break the Body of Christ beyond repair. We take smooth-faced young men out of their mother's kitchens to teach them how to march blindly into death, how to destroy what they do not know, how to hate what they have not seen. We make victims of the victors themselves. We call the psychological maiming, the physical squandering, the spiritual distortion of the nation's most vulnerable defenders "defense." We turn their parents and sweethearts and children into the aged, the widowed, and the orphaned before their time. "We make a wasteland and call it peace," the Roman poet Seneca wrote with miserable insight.

THERE IS A SEASON

When the car stopped, we found ourselves in the front courtyard of a huge marble building. Fronted by narrow marble steps and great columned portico, it had all the marks of a standard Roman Catholic installation. Except that we were not in Rome. We were in a convent in Damascus run by a feisty old nun, Regina, a sister of St. Basil. It was a classic institution confronted by a very current situation.

The four sisters there work with Iraqi refugees. "Four thousand Iraqi refugees a day come to Syria," Sr. Regina told us. Whatever the daily figure, Archbishop Avak Asadourian told us later, more than a million Iraqis have fled to Syria for protection from U.S. bombs and their newly generated internecine strife.

The sisters feed the refugees three times a week on fresh soups and casseroles, vegetables, bread and meat donated by both the members of the parish and their Muslim friends around them. The people come with old pots and pans, the sisters fill them to the brim. The people take the food back for the rest of the family to make meals and home and family life as normal as possible in a totally abnormal situation.

Four sisters, older but undaunted, collect clothes for them, manage a medical clinic to care for them and try to get them housing. "Come and see them," she said.

I was a bit reluctant to go with her, afraid to embarrass them, concerned that the very presence of Americans could break the thin thread of strength that gave them a last semblance of dignity. But since she and I had made a personal contact—she a Basilian, I a Benedictine—she pushed me out into the midst of them in the inner courtyard where they were all watching us through the windows. I could hardly get out the door. They pressed around me, all talking at once. We were Americans and they knew it.

The rest of the time is almost a blur, meaning I don't know what happened in what order. But I do know what happened. I looked into their faces while the translator pointed each of them out: This one's son had been killed, these lost their homes, this one saw her family shot to death by American soldiers, these here have nowhere to go. The list was endless. "I am so sorry," I said to them. "I am so sorry this happened to you. Many, many Americans tried to stop this. All I can do is apologize to you from the center of my heart for the millions of Americans who are concerned for you."

"And what good does that do?" a young teenager said, a sharp edge to her voice. Suddenly, a woman pushed forward from the back of the jostling crowd, big black eyes fixed on me intently. She turned to the translator for help. "I accept your apology," she said quietly. "I accept your love." Then she put her arms around me, kissed me firmly on the cheek, put her head on my shoulder and began to cry. And so did I. The rest of the group pressed tightly against us, all of them with tears on their faces.

I had never seen the faces of my victims before and they had not seen the face of the enemy who was not an enemy. It was a profound moment for all of us.

"FROM WHERE I STAND," NCRONLINE.ORG
NOVEMBER 16, 2006

It is time to remember that the just-war theory is just that. It is a theory that, at the very least, is poorly applied or that—given the nature of modern warfare—is clearly inadequate. George Bernard Shaw taught that reasonable people adapt themselves to the world and that unreasonable ones persist in trying to adapt the world to themselves. "Therefore," he wrote, "all progress depends on the unreasonable."

SALT MAGAZINE
MAY 1992

However benign and enlightened the world may now claim to be, the fact remains that politicians use religion as a fan to inflame the ire of people who have too many daily worries to even think about arguing politics but who will gladly die to preserve their religion.

At the same time, the forgotten reality is that every religion teaches peace and respect for the other. And that truth has a way of seeping up and spilling over into the human psyche even when religions do everything they can to avoid it.

Nevertheless, in the name of religion, radical
fundamentalists of every stripe have gone on arguing
the union of God's will, the purpose of civil society
and their own theological views. Christian states have
persecuted other Christians as well as non-Christians.
Theocratic states have excluded non-believers from the
body politic. We have all sinned.

Obviously, religion itself is not really the problem.
But, from where I stand, until religion is part of the
answer, until religions everywhere refuse to be used to
advance the very secular ends of power and greed and
control and domination that the secular world seeks,
then religion will continue to be the hot ashes under
every conflict.

"FROM WHERE I STAND," NCRONLINE.ORG
JUNE 24, 2003

When I have really learned to suffer with the other—
the poor, the voiceless, the marginalized, the people
without power—I'll begin to see a whole new world.
I'll begin to see the violence around me and in me. I'll
begin to see the need to refuse to cooperate with it.

There is no doubt: it takes courage to face down
a violent generation without becoming like them. It
takes courage to stop violence by refusing to continue
it. It takes courage to absorb the amount of punishment
required to rob the brutal of the joy of their brutality
and to turn the tide of this senselessness.

The little people who faced the dogs in Selma to gain their humanity, the tiny women who climbed the fences of nuclear installations to pray for their dismantling, the little groups who sign petition after petition to stop planetary pollution, the little boats that obstruct the wanton killing of dolphins and whales, the myriad little people who refuse to be willing victims of an age more given to death than to life—these are seeds of a new human consciousness, a new global soul.

ACTIVE NONVIOLENCE
FOREWORD

Opposite: Joan Chittister in front of
Saint Mary's Church, Erie, PA.
Photograph by Rick Klein.
Courtesy Benetvision.

CHAPTER 6

WHAT IS SIN?

The ancients talked about the "gift of tears," the grace of sorrow for sin. Sin is not a popular concept these days, and sorrow is even more suspect in this culture. "We don't sin; we make mistakes," the respondents to a study of contemporary Christian beliefs report. We do not, the modern version holds, need to weep either for our own brokenness or for the damage we have done to others because, unfortunate as it may be, it was beyond our conscious control. As a result of thinking like that, we simply limp along from "mistake" to "mistake," taking responsibility for little and having concern for less. In the end, then, we may fail to identify the patterns of our lives that have us retracing ourselves in a series of steadily decreasing circles until we stand trapped in our own unreflective and unrewarding behaviors. We ignore the call to holiness in ourselves that consistent and constant struggle invites us to require. Worse, we ignore the effects of our lack of ethical principles on others.

THERE IS A SEASON

It is not that sin is not sin. It is simply that sin is not the end of the world—and, in fact, may actually be the beginning of a number of things that can hardly be gained any other way in life, but without which life is a pitiful place. A bout with greed may be precisely what teaches us the freedom of poverty. A struggle with lust may well be what, in the end, teaches us about the real nature of love. A strong dose of anger may be what it takes to teach us the beauty of gentleness.

There are, in other words, a number of things to be learned from sin. One is compassion. The other is understanding. The third is humility. The fourth is perception. Without the ability to own our own sins, these qualities are all hard to come by indeed.

Sin gears us to suffer with those who suffer from the folly of their weaknesses because we have smarted from the folly of our own. Once we can admit our own sins, once we face those things in ourselves which if ever brought to light would be our social downfall, we can companion those for whom the darkness of night has not been so kind. Sin enables us to understand the murderer, to deal justly with the criminal, to control the passion for blood that masks the sins of the righteous with a patina of virtue.

In the end, however, it may be humility and perception that are the best consequences—the intended consequences—of the surfeit of sin. Humility not only identifies us with the human race and confirms the earthiness of the human condition, but it erodes the very basis for hierarchy as well. Humility knows that there are no lords-of-the-manor at all; no ones of us at all entitled to subject the rest of us; nobody at all good enough or pure enough to evaluate the rest of us. We are all in struggle. We are all attempting to kill within ourselves the very toxins that poison the human race in general. We are all at the mercy of the God of mercy. We can all learn something from one another.

What we need to kill in life may not be sin at all. What we may really need to avoid like the plague may be the temptation to a bare and brutal sinlessness that threatens us with heartlessness, the greatest sin of all.

THERE IS A SEASON

Life's major problem does not lie in choosing good from evil. That's obvious and easy. No, life's real problem comes in choosing good from good. What's the answer? That's also easy: when values are in conflict, always choose the higher one.

IN A HIGH SPIRITUAL SEASON

When Pope John XXIII talked about "the signs of the times,"—poverty, nuclearism, sexism—I began to read these signs with a new conscience and with a new sense of religious life in mind. Most of all, I began to read the Scriptures through another lens. Who was this Jesus who "consorted with sinners" and cured on the Sabbath? Most of all, who was I who purported to be following him while police dogs snarled at black children and I made sure not to be late for prayer or leave my monastery after dark? What was "the prophetic dimension" of the Church supposed to be about if not the concerns of the prophets: the widows, the orphans, the foreigners and the broken, vulnerable, of every society?

We prayed the psalms five times a day for years, but I had failed to hear them. What I heard in those early years of religious life was the need to pray. I forgot to hear what I was praying. Then, one day I realized just how secular the psalmist was in comparison to the religious standards in which I had been raised: "You, O God, do see trouble and grief.…You are the helper of the weak," the psalmist argues. No talk of fuzzy, warm religion here. This was life raw and hard. This was what God called to account. (Psalm 10:14) This was sin.

When the Latin American bishops talked about a "fundamental option for the poor," I began to see the poor in our inner-city neighborhood for the first time. When Rosa Parks and Martin Luther King Jr. finally stood up in Birmingham, Alabama, I stood up, too. I was ready now. Like the blind man of Mark's gospel, I could finally see. The old question had been answered. The sin to be repented, amended, eradicated was the great systemic sin against God's little ones. For that kind of sin, in my silence, I had become deeply guilty.

I had new questions then but they were far more energizing than the ones before them. I began to look more closely at what "living a good life" could possibly mean in a world that was so full of suffering, so full of greed.

I began to realize that "a good life" had something do with making life good for other people. Slowly, slowly I began to arrive at the oldest Catholic truth of them all: all of life is good and sanctity does not consist in denying that. Sanctity consists in making life good for everyone whose life we touch.

SPIRITUAL QUESTIONS FOR THE 21ST CENTURY

The question, "What is sin?" had changed my life completely. I came to understand that selfishness, self-centeredness, and the kind of self-indulgence that is bought at the expense of the other was the real essence of sin. The private little wrestling matches, the pitfalls that come and go with the process of personal development, were all part of all our secret struggles to resist the predisposition to sin that is part of being human. Those were all part of the growing up process, yes, but it was not of the real essence of either sin or sanctity. Sanctity had far more to do with building up the reign of God here and now for everyone. All the saints were "sinners" in the narcissistic sense of the word. But all the saints were also those who overturned tables in every temple of every system in which exploiting the little ones of the world was one of the givens of the social game. Since God lives in us all, the destruction of the other has got to be a sin against God.

SPIRITUAL QUESTIONS FOR THE 21ST CENTURY

The nice thing about guilt is that it proves that we are still alive. If we can still feel moral angst, we can feel everything else in life, too. The first sign of healthy guilt is that we never feel guilty for the wrong things. Guilt always has something to do with failing to recognize my creaturehood or hurting someone else.

The second sign of healthy guilt is that it is not exaggerated. Spiritual vision is the ability to see things as they are. Some of our struggles are serious; some of them are not. Some of our moral arm-wrestling matches of life are long-standing and need to be uprooted; some of them are only momentary breakdowns in an otherwise well-ordered soul.

The third sign of healthy guilt is that we do something about it and put the situation behind us. The purpose of guilt always is simply to enable us to recognize where we are failing the coming of the reign of God so that we can do better the next time. Its purpose is not to leave us wallowing in the past. Never to feel guilty for anything I've done is to be a spiritual child. Always to feel guilty for things without substance is to be a spiritual invalid.

In Search of Belief

"*The sins* of others are before our eyes; our own are behind our backs," the Roman poet Seneca wrote. The terrible truth has been spoken. We hide from others and from ourselves those things about ourselves which, if we knew them, could save us. If we admitted our arrogance, faced our dishonesties, named our weaknesses—at least to ourselves—we would be consumed with kindness. We would know what God knows: that there is no one who is not struggling with the same kinds of things we are. There is no one who does not need and deserve our care.

THE MONASTIC WAY

Shakespeare, in the classic "Hamlet," says about everything we need to know about the tension between what is goodness—and what is really goodness. In Act I, Scene V, Hamlet says, "That one may smile and smile and be a villain."

The insight, at first sight, seems obvious but the trick for us is to avoid the pitfall that comes with virtue gone bad.

When the Church protects pedophile priests in order to save the Church rather than the children, the instinct may be understandable but it is not right. When Jesuit Dan Berrigan spent years in jail for protesting nuclear weapons in order to call the attention of the country to the devastating effects of nuclearism on children everywhere, here as well in war zones, goodness, generosity, love glowed into a flame seen round the world.

Down deep, we always know the difference between the good and the really good. Down deep we can always smell spoiled virtue even when we can't see it. In a society thick with corporate wealth and poor on social services, we can see the distance between goodness and greatness, between compassion that is real and the kind of humanity that is rare.

THE MONASTIC WAY

The world I live in, not the perfume of incense and the sweet words of prayer, is the stuff of my sanctification. To ignore the suffering around me in the name of being realistic or reasonable or objective about it—as women are repeatedly told to be—makes me culpable not simply of the situation itself but of what scholastic theologians call "giving full consent of the will." I see it, I think about it, I consider it and decide to do nothing about it at all. I am too busy. It is too large a problem for one person to do anything about. The people involved are too questionable. Or, most commonly, it's not my responsibility. Compassion says yes, it is.

HEART OF FLESH

Whatever the price to be paid, whatever the cost to ourselves—our public comfort, our social status—if the banality of evil in this time is to be confronted, we, you and I, must come to understand that what the world is really missing in its immersion in the evil of mediocrity is us.

The banality of evil rests on our bland unawareness that we are the only thing between it and success.

The fact is that every holocaust begins—or ends—with me.

BLESSED ARE YOU
LENT 2006

To support the poor without devoting ourselves to eliminating the causes of their poverty is neither justice nor patience. Ministry without advocacy is no ministry at all. It simply perpetuates a sinful system.

Justice is a condition of the heart as much as it is a social situation. When we stop taking injustice for granted, it will cease to exist. As it is, we assume that because sin is human that it must also be allowed to become an acceptable part of the civic or political arena.

To counsel patience in the face of human misery is to deny the will of God for all creation. It is one thing to endure evil while we work for good; it is another thing entirely to assume that the evil we face is all we can ever expect.

BECOMING FULLY HUMAN

Between life and death it is for all of us to do one blazing act of good—however small it may seem at the time. Life is the opportunity to speak one great truth in the face of one great lie. It may seem that no one hears it. It may seem that nothing changes. But not to speak—that is the real sin. Then, smallness is the lot even of the great. Only the doing of justice is a good enough excuse to be born.

CALLED TO QUESTION

In the environment that spawned World War II, Gertrude Stein said that the most important thing for Germans to learn was disobedience. In 1973 an American sociologist, Gerda Lederer, did a large-scale comparative study of authoritarianism in West German and American adolescents. Authoritarianism—the willingness to submit to authority and the need to dominate others—had been a pre-war hallmark of Nazi Germany. Prepared by Bismarck's military regime and nourished by Hitler through the Nazi Youth Corps, this disposition to blind obedience to official command was later pointed to by social psychologists to explain the compliance of German Christians in the Jewish holocaust.

The astonishing conclusion of Lederer's study was that by 1973 German teenagers had become even less authoritarian than their American counterparts even though they had much further to come in their development of anti-authoritarian principles.

What may be even more telling are the findings of Stanley Milgram's eight-year study. Nearly two-thirds of the participants in a study to determine the degree to which subjects were willing to inflict pain on another individual simply because they had been directed to do so by an authority figure complied completely. They never questioned either the reasons or the results of their action. They simply followed orders on the assumption that if they had been told by an official that their cooperation in this violence was necessary, then indeed it must be.

To make matters worse, D.C. Brock researched the relationship between religious beliefs and obedience to destructive command and concluded: "Religious beliefs and behaviors are related to obedience. A clear trend of refusal to yield to authority was noted in non-believers. Moderate believers were consistently high in the delivery of shock, but believers were the most obedient, delivering more shock than any other group."

Every day people that the churches have educated go quietly and serenely to factories where they assemble warheads, to laboratories where they increase the megaton capacity of our arsenals, to boardrooms where they vote to increase our "defense" capabilities.

The role of the religious community in such a culture is surely a clear one. It is of course to pray for peace, not to cajole God to save us from our own insane sinfulness but to make ourselves receptive to God's in-breaking in our lives and culture. It is as well to be centers of peace where strangers can become sisters or brothers in Christ. It is, finally to become models of disobedience.

Erich Fromm describes the "revolutionary personality" as a person who is independent, who has the capacity to identify deeply with humanity and who has the ability to disobey in the interest of more fundamental values. The prophets, Christ, the early Christians would understand the role completely. It is up to the religious of this day, who take a public vow of obedience to God, to reclaim and recall a conforming world to the burning burden of that promise.

WOMEN, MINISTRY AND THE CHURCH

If there is a major problem in spirituality today, it may be that we do not do enough to form Christians for resistance to evil. We form them for patient endurance and for civil conformity. We form them to be "good" but not necessarily to be "holy." In the doing of it, we make compliant Christians rather than courageous ones, as if bearing evil were more important than confronting it. We go on separating life into parts, one spiritual, one not.

This tension between what is profane and what is spiritual makes all the difference between a holy life and a pious life.

CALLED TO QUESTION

Sin changes with age. In youth it is born out of impulse; in later years it is based in calculation. The first stage requires the ability to discriminate and the development of control. It's a period of experimentation that can end in wisdom. But at a later stage, when we have really come to "know good from evil," sin requires that we review the entire value system that drives us. Something has gone seriously awry. And in the end it is not just what our sin does to other people that counts; it is what sin does to us that matters deeply, as well.

LIVING WELL

Opposite: Joan Chittister with her mother, Loretta, upon graduating with a Master of Arts degree from University of Notre Dame, 1968. Courtesy Benetvision.

CHAPTER 7

𝒲HEN IS IT
TIME FOR WOMEN?

The fact is that I am a feminist precisely because I am a Catholic—not as a reaction to what is wrong about the Church but as a response to what is right about the Church. My Christian feminist commitment to the equality, dignity, and humanity of all persons and my determination to change structures to enable equality does not come as a result of rejecting what I see as bad in the Church. It comes as an inevitable recognition of what I see as the great, the magnetizing, the empowering, the energizing good that is inherent for women in the Church and promised for women in the Church, even when I cannot see it yet being brought to fullness, even in the Church.

SOJOURNERS MAGAZINE, JULY 1987

Is it possible for a person to be a good feminist and a good Christian at the same time? The answer is, How is it possible to be a good Christian without being a good feminist?

A feminist spirituality would change marriage, change society, change Church, change the very definition of sanctity. Those patterns touch the core of Christianity as we know it. Those things call us to the Christianity of the Jesus who preceded the patriarchal Church. Those concepts would turn the world upside down. They are holy-making ideas for our time. No wonder they threaten the system so much.

HEART OF FLESH

One of my favorite remembrances of grade school is the May altar. Everyday we said our prayers in front of it; every day we loaded it down with fresh flowers purloined from every yard along the way to school. It was a child's way of growing into the idea that heaven was not without a mother's protection and a woman's care.

This culture has substituted machoism and power for feminine concern and gentleness. Maybe that's why all the violence of our time is such a shock to our systems. It is clearly time for May altars again. We need to be shocked at the savagery we have come to call *defense*.

IN A HIGH SPIRITUAL SEASON

To design the doctrines of the Church on salvation, sexuality, marriage, family, and sin—all of which affect the lives of women equally but differently than they do the lives of men—without formative input from women themselves, conveys positions that are incomplete as well as arrogant.

THE PAPACY AND THE PEOPLE OF GOD

In diocese after diocese, Catholic parishes are being merged, closed, or served by retired priests or married male deacons designed to keep the Church male, whether it is ministering or not. The number of priests is declining, the number of Catholics is increasing, and the number of lay ministers being certified is rising in every academic system despite the fact that their services are being rejected.

Clearly, the Catholic Church is changing even while it reasserts its changelessness. But static resistance is a far cry from the dynamism of the early Church. Prisca, Lydia, Thecla, Phoebe, and hundreds of women like them opened house churches, walked as disciples of Paul, "constrained him," the scripture says, to serve a given region, instructed people in the faith, and ministered to the fledgling Christian communities with no apology, no argument, and no tricky theological shell games about whether they were ministering *in persona Christi* or *in nomini Christi.*

So what is to be done at a time like this, when what is being sought and what is possible are two different things? To what are we to give our energy when we are told no energy is wanted?

The answer is discipleship. The fact is that we cannot possibly have a renewed priesthood unless we have a renewed discipleship around us and in us as well. The temptation is to become weary in the apparently fruitless search for office. But the call is to become recommitted to the essential, the ancient, and the authentic demands of discipleship.

Christian discipleship is a very dangerous thing. It is about living in this world the way that Jesus the Christ lived in his—touching lepers, raising donkeys from ditches on Sabbath days, questioning the unquestionable and—consorting with women! Discipleship implies a commitment to leave nets and homes, positions and securities, lordship and legalities to be now—in our own world—what the Christ was for his. Discipleship is prepared to fly in the face of a world bent only on maintaining its own ends whatever the cost.

SOJOURNERS MAGAZINE, JAN/FEB 2002

That the definition of women by men is limiting and false is difficult enough. The effects of these very definitions on the development of women are even worse. If psychology has taught us nothing else, it is at least clear now that the oppressed internalize the message of the oppressor; that people live down to their stunted expectations. Inferiority, in other words, is learned from the standard setters of a society whose access to the schools and courts and legislatures of a people have the power to define the rights of others. It is precisely about the nature and possibilities of women that women must educate the Church, or humanity may never come to know the fullness of God's creation. If women had no other ministry than this, the world and the Church would be different tomorrow.

WINDS OF CHANGE

The Theology of Domination says, in essence, that men and women are created out of the same substance but that men are superior; that God, in effect, made some humans more human than other humans; that some people are in charge of other people and can do whatever is necessary to maintain that God-given right and responsibility. The social implications of such theology is serious. If God built inequality into the human race, then it is acceptable to argue that some races are unequal to other races. It is clear that the subjugation of whole peoples by another is natural and even desirable. It is obvious that the use of force against other nations and cultures which are considered inferior can be justified and embarked on as a way of life. Even in democracies, some people may be denied the vote because they are inferior, untouchable, unacceptable to those who have gained power, either by force or by natural rights.

The theology of domination makes sexism, racism and militarism of a piece. It brings into clear focus the role of religion in world order, development and peace.

WOMEN'S STUDIES ENCYCLOPEDIA

I'm a thinker, I'm a reader, and I discovered that the early Church had deaconesses. But when the Church restored the diaconate ten years ago they restored it for males only. Now when I want to cite the prejudice of the Church against women, I don't need to talk about ordination to the priesthood. All I have to ask is, "Why can't women be ordained as deacons?" That's where the objections waiver: tradition, theology, experience, history. The institution of the permanent diaconate says very clearly that women are not wanted. It's not right. It's not right. Sexism is a sin and it must be repented. It's that simple.

Don't tell me how wonderful women are until you can sweep a television camera around the congress or the board of directors or the parish staff or council and show a number of women equal to the number of men. Don't tell me how wonderful women are until you think that our values and our ideas and our conclusions are important to decision-making.

TODAY'S PARISH MAGAZINE
OCTOBER 1984
INTERVIEW WITH CAROL CLARK

Clearly, a great deal more will have to change before we will be able to tell with certainty that God decided to "make them in God's own image" and so "male and female God made them." Some important dimensions are lacking, without which we will be very unlikely to progress.

The spiritual concept to God must be reclaimed. The continuing emphasis on God as father, rather than on God as spirit, as life, as essence, as all being, is very subtly limiting of women and very clearly controlling of them. If God is male, then males are truly closer to God and femaleness becomes the undivine other, the leftover, the unknown, the unholy. And, of course, the subordinate.

Maleness has become the new idolatry, the golden calf we worship in our churches and confirm in our social structures. The feminine dimensions of God go unnoted and unknown in a world that has appropriated the warrior God to its militaristic self but has completely overlooked the birthing God who gives all of us everything we need for life, if we will only distribute it. Even to hint at the possibility that the generation of life is an exclusively male prerogative, by arguing that God must be seen as father because God is the generator of life, is to participate in embarrassingly bad biology. Heresy, perhaps.

We will certainly be what we worship. But we worship only half the reality of life. Of course God is a personal God. Of course God is father. But God is much more than that, as the language of the Church has always maintained. We have traditionally called God rock, fire, dove and lion. We must begin to ask ourselves why we never call God mother.

As long as our image of God remains so narrow, so will our experience of God in the world. So will our vision of Church.

NOTRE DAME MAGAZINE
WINTER 1991-92

There must be something in the male psyche of the Church that insists on projecting onto the female its fears of itself. God-language itself unmasks the fragmentation in the Church's understanding of God.

It is time for the Church to become whole. It is time for the papacy to lead us out of such tangled theological morass, back to the Jesus of lepers and outcasts and women, of beseeching women and proclaiming women and ministering women, of women with reckless faith, and fearless presence and interminable fidelity.

We need a Pentecost papacy in the next millennium that can hear the many voices of women—each speaking in her own tongue—and understand them.

THE PAPACY AND THE PEOPLE OF GOD

Clearly, a woman's real problem lies just as much in being too revered as it does in being too reviled. To be revered means to meet the expectations of those who really have respect in a society. To be revered means, then, to be allowed to be only half of who you are. It is not a simple choice: To be what other people want you to be gets approval. "I'm not a feminist but..." I said for years, eager to keep my credentials as "good sister," "nice woman." Then one day I noticed that I was for equal pay, equal rights, equal representation, equal protection under the law and a theology as respectful of women as channels of grace as it was of men. There was no way out. I could no longer exclude myself from the ranks of those who believed in the full implications of the fact that women were also rays of God's energy on earth.

"I don't want you anyplace near my daughter," a woman said to me. "I want her to be a good wife and mother, not a feminist." As if the two are irreconcilable. But the situation was clear: To be what you are, to say what you think, to do what you need to do to be your most developed self means to risk rejection. The remnants of that kind of social mentality lurk everywhere yet. Little girls still get told to be "little ladies," meaning docile and quiet when they may most need to learn to be assertive and loud. Adolescent girls still get catcalled down one street and up another. Adult women still leave marriages after years of disapproval and they still leave Churches, too, after hearing throughout their entire lives that even God has rejected them. The problem becomes how to keep self-respect in a society that claims to revere you but does not respect you.

THE STORY OF RUTH

I am not impressed by people who say they are pro-life but who don't want to pay taxes to provide housing and food and education and healthcare for those who need them. That's not pro-life; it's pro-birth. This society needs to make life livable for the least fortunate before it condemns people who, for whatever reason, believe they cannot bring a life into the world.

THE SUN MAGAZINE
JUNE 2007
INTERVIEW WITH JAMES KULLANDER

In order to create a feminist environment, questions have got to be in vogue. Nothing can be off limits to discussion, to exploration, to possibility. Questions are not an indication of chaos, they are an indication of concern. They measure the degree of interest a person brings to a subject. They alert us to significance.

Questions, then, become key to the development of an open mind because a question opens a flood-gate of possible answers.

To question present assumptions requires faith in the God of the future as well as respect for the God of the past.

Feminism confronts the world with openness to differences and values them. The stranger becomes the bearer of a new kind of competency, another kind of effectiveness, a treasure-house of possibility. Feminism challenges the world to trust again.

HEART OF FLESH

When I was eight years old the parish novena to Our Lady of Perpetual Help, with its incense and hymns and litanies and crowded pews, had a much more powerful effect on me than the early morning masses that the priest said in the dark and empty church every day. I loved it when the congregation sang "O Sanctissima, O Piissima, Virgo Mater Maria" till it rang off the rafters and throbbed against the walls of the church.

Most of all I loved the litany of Our Lady's titles, the meanings of which I could not even imagine: Mary, House of Gold, we prayed. Mary, Morning Star. Mary, Gate of Heaven. Mary. Mary. Mary. Whatever you needed, whatever was missing from life Mary could get, the people believed. Whatever all the words meant I did not begin to know but one thing was sure: Mary was powerful in the reign of God and Mary was a woman.

PAX CHRISTI USA MAGAZINE
SUMMER 1989

The Coronation of Mary is the unfulfilled mystery of the rosary. As long as any woman anywhere is denied access to God, or status in life, or equality with men, as long as any of the little ones anywhere are deprived of respect and position, then Mary's place in heaven is mocked. The Coronation of Mary as Queen of Heaven is a call to see equality as the fullness of the will of God.

IN PURSUIT OF PEACE

Feminist spirituality demands that women become adults. It's that simple. They must learn to take responsibility for their ideas. They must, if they believe that the Holy Spirit works in everyone, begin to speak their truth themselves. At whatever the cost. They have no right to hide behind men, to manipulate men, to get what they want by wheedling and whining rather than by claiming it for themselves honestly and strongly.

I have a notion that we'll know the world has become healthy—has become holy—when we no longer think in terms of either women or men. The world—science, religion, politics—has stereotyped women for so long that it has ceased to see either women or men as real individuals.

CALLED TO QUESTION

SELECTED BIBLIOGRAPHY

BOOKS BY JOAN CHITTISTER

Becoming Fully Human: The Greatest Glory of God, Sheed & Ward, 2005.

Called to Question: A Spiritual Memoir, Sheed & Ward, 2004.

The Fire in These Ashes: A Spirituality of Contemporary Religious Life, Sheed & Ward, 1995.

The Friendship of Women: The Hidden Tradition of the Bible, BlueBridge, 2006. (Revised edition of *The Friendship of Women: A Spiritual Tradition*, Benetvision, 2000).

The Gift of Years: Growing Older Gracefully, BlueBridge, 2008.

Heart of Flesh: A Feminist Spirituality for Women and Men, Wm. B. Eerdmans, 1998.

Illuminated Life: Monastic Wisdom for Seekers of Light, Orbis Books, 2000.

In the Heart of the Temple: My Spiritual Vision for Today's World, Blue-Bridge, 2004. (Revised edition of *New Designs*. Benetvision, 2002).

In a High Spiritual Season, Liguori/Triumph Books, 1995.

In Search of Belief, Liguori Publications, 1999. Revised edition, 2006.

Life Ablaze: A Woman's Novena, Sheed & Ward, 2000. (Revised edition of booklet by Benetvision, 1997).

Listen With the Heart: Sacred Moments in Everyday Life, Sheed & Ward, 2003.

Living Well: Scriptural Reflections for Every Day, Orbis Books, 2000.

Passion for Life: Fragments of the Face of God, Orbis Books, 1996.

The Psalms: Meditations for Every Day of the Year, The Crossroad Publishing Co., 1996.

Scarred by Struggle, Transformed by Hope, Wm. B. Eerdmans, 2003.

Seeing With Our Souls: Monastic Wisdom for Every Day, Sheed & Ward, 2002.

The Rule of Benedict: Insights for the Ages, The Crossroad Publishing Co., 1992.

The Story of Ruth: Twelve Moments in Every Woman's Life, Wm. B. Eerdmans, 2000.

The Ten Commandments: Laws of the Heart, Orbis Books, 2006.

The Tent of Abraham, Stories of Hope and Peace for Jews, Christians and Muslims, Chittister, Chishti, Waskow, Beacon Press, 2006.

The Way We Were: A Story of Conversion and Renewal, Orbis Books, 2005.

There Is a Season, Orbis Books, 1995.

Twelve Steps to Inner Freedom: Humility Revisited, Benetvision, 2003.

Welcome to the Wisdom of the World, Wm. B. Eerdmans, 2007.

25 Windows into the Soul: Praying With the Psalms, Benetvision, 2007.

Winds of Change, Sheed & Ward, 1986.

Wisdom Distilled from the Daily: Living the Rule of St. Benedict Today, Harper & Row, 1990.

Women, Church and Ministry, Paulist Press, 1983.

OTHER COLLECTIONS

Collections from *The Monastic Way*, a monthly publication with daily reflections, by Joan Chittister, www.benetvision.org.

40-Day Journey with Joan Chittister, Beverly Lanzetta, ed., Augsburg Books, 2007.

Spiritual Questions for the 21st Century: Essays in Honor of Joan D. Chittister, Mary Hembrow-Snyder, ed., Orbis Books, 2001.

Sources and Permissions

The compiler wishes to express her gratitude to the following for granting permission to reproduce material of which they are the publisher or copyright holder.

Reprinted with permission of Wm. B. Eerdmans, Grand Rapids, MI:

Excerpts from the following: *Heart of Flesh* by Joan Chittister © 1998; *Scarred by Struggle, Transformed by Hope* by Joan Chittister © 2003; *The Story of Ruth* by Joan Chittister © 2000; *Welcome to the Wisdom of the World* by Joan Chittister © 2007.

Reprinted with permission of Orbis Books, Maryknoll, NY:

Excerpts from the following: *Illuminated Life* by Joan Chittister © 2000; *Living Well* by Joan Chittister © 2000; *The Papacy and the People of God*, Gary MacEoin, ed. © 1998; *Spiritual Questions for the Twenty-First Century*, Hembrow-Snyder ed. © 2001; *There Is a Season* by Joan Chittister © 1995.

Reprinted with permission of BlueBridge, New York, NY:

Excerpts from the following: *The Friendship of Women* by Joan Chittister © 2006 (usage in Canada by permission of Novalis, Ottawa, Ontario, Canada); *The Gift of Years* by Joan Chittister © 2008 (usage in Canada by permission of Novalis, Ottawa, Ontario, Canada; usage in United Kingdom and Ireland by permission of Darton Longman & Todd, London); *In the Heart of the Temple* by Joan Chittister © 2004 (usage in Canada by permission of Novalis, Ottawa, Ontario, Canada; usage in United Kingdom and Europe by permission of SPCK, London).

Reprinted with permission of Sheed & Ward, Franklin, WI, an imprint of Rowman & Littlefield Publishers, Inc., Lanham, MD:

Excerpts from the following: *Becoming Fully Human* by Joan Chittister © 2005; *Called to Question* by Joan Chittister © 2004; *Listen With the Heart* by Joan Chittister © 2003; *Seeing with Our Souls* by Joan Chittister © 2002.

Reprinted with permission of Liguori Publications, Liguori, MO:

Excerpts from *In Search of Belief* by Joan Chittister © 1999, 2006.

Other sources reprinted with permission:

Excerpts from the following: *God at 2000*, Marcus Borg & Ross Mackenzie, ed. Morehouse Publishing, Harrisburg, PA © 2000; Afterword for *Grace Is Everywhere: Reflections of an Aspiring Monk* by James Stephen Behrens, ACTA Publications, Chicago, IL © 1999; *In Pursuit of Peace: Praying the Rosary through the Psalms* by Joan Chittister, Pax Christi USA & Benetvision © joint publication with Pax Christi 2003, www.paxchristiusa.org; Foreword for *Praying with the Benedictines: A Window on the Cloister,* by Guerric DeBona, Paulist Press, New York/Mahwah, NJ © 2007; *The Psalms* by Joan Chittister, Crossroad Publishing Co., New York © 1996; *What Does It Mean to Be Human?* gathered by Frederick Franck, Janis Roze and Richard Connolly, Circumstantial Productions in cooperation with Unesco Institute for Education, Nyack, NY © 1998.

Reprinted with grateful acknowledgement:

Excerpts from the following: Foreword for *Active Nonviolence: A Way of Personal Peace* by Gerald A. Vanderhaar, Twenty-Third Publications, Mystic, CT © 1990; "Amos' Message for Today's World," *Liguorian* Magazine, April 1995; Interview by editors, "Part III: The Balance of Time: Spirituality to Sustain a Life of Ministry," *Sojourners* Magazine, August-September, 1987; Interview by James Kullander, "Be Not Silent: Sister Joan Chittister Speaks Out on War, Feminism, and the Catholic Church," *The Sun* Magazine, June 2007; "Beauty, Bridge to Justice," Benetvision 2000 Calendar; *Being Catholic Now* by Kerry Kennedy, Crown Publishers, New York © 2008; *Blessed Are You: Overcoming Evil with Good,* Benetvision, Lent 2006; Interview by Art Winter, "Contemplation, Everyone?" *Praying* Magazine 1991; "A Dangerous Discipleship," *Sojourners* Magazine, January-February, 2002; "Ezekiel: Seer of the Unseen," *Liguorian*, November, 1995; "From Contemplation to Justice," *Radical Grace* Newspaper, April-May-June 2006; "From Where I Stand," NCRonline, June 24, 2003; "From Where I Stand," NCRonline, July 8, 2003; "From Where I Stand," NCRonline, April 10, 2006; "From Where I Stand," NCRonline, Nov. 16, 2006; "The Healing Pool of Bethsaida: A Model for Ministry," *The Journal of the Catholic Women's Network*, August, 1993; *How Shall We Live?* Kownacki, ed. Benetvision (out of print); "I Need a Hero," Beliefnet.org., Dec. 9, 2000; *In a Dark Wood*, Linda Jones & Sophie Stones, ed. Augsburg Fortress Publishers, Minneapolis, MN © 2003; *In a High Spiritual Season,* Liguori/Triumph Books, 1995; Interview by Carol Clark, "Joan Chittister: Prophet for Peace," *Today's Parish*, Oct. 1984; "Isaiah: Steadfast in the Face of Adversity," *Liguorian* Magazine, August 1995; "Leading the Way: To Go Where There Is No Road and Leave a Path," *Ignatius Loyola—Spirit and Practice for Today: Key Readings for Busy People*, Martin Scroope, ed. Loyola Institute, Sydney 2002; "Liturgy: To Comfort or to Liberate?" *Pastoral Music*, October, 1995; *Living in the Breath of the Spirit,* Kownacki, ed. Benetvision 1999; *The Monastic Way,* Benetvision; Interview by editors, "Peace is Worth Getting Riled About," *U.S. Catholic*, September 1988; Interview by editors, "Prayer Ought to Disturb the Peace," *SALT* Magazine, March 1989; "Spirituality for the Long Haul," *Compass* Magazine, May-June,

1992; Interview by Rev. Joseph J. Driscoll, "Spirituality: Theology Walking," *Vision* Magazine, October 1996; "Theology of Domination," *Women's Studies Encyclopedia,* Volume 3, Helen Tierney, ed. © 1986, published by Greenwood Publishing Group, Inc., Westport, CT; "There Just Aren't Any Just Wars Anymore," *SALT* Magazine, May 1992; "Viewpoint Woman: Litanies and Village Women and God and Us," *Pax Christi USA* Magazine, Summer 1989; "Viewpoint Woman: Transforming Action," *Pax Christi USA* Magazine, June 1985; *Winds of Change,* Sheed & Ward, 1986; "Why I Stay," by Joan Chittister, *Lutheran Woman Today,* October 1996; *25 Windows into the Soul,* Kownacki, ed. Benetvision 2007; *Wisdom Distilled from the Daily: Living the Rule of St. Benedict Today,* by Joan Chittister, Harper Collins, San Francisco © 1990; "A Woman's Place," *Notre Dame Magazine,* Winter 1991-92; "Yesterday's Dangerous Vision: Christian Feminism in the Catholic Church," *Sojourners* Magazine, July 1987.